Discipline
WITH
Dignity

4TH EDITION

ASCD MEMBER BOOK

Many ASCD members received this book as a
member benefit upon its initial release.

Learn more at www.ascd.org/memberbooks

Alexandria, Virginia USA

Discipline WITH Dignity

4TH EDITION

How to Build Responsibility, Relationships, and Respect in Your Classroom

RICHARD L. CURWIN

ALLEN N. MENDLER

BRIAN D. MENDLER

1703 N. Beauregard St. • Alexandria, VA 22311-1714 USA
Phone: 800-933-2723 or 703-578-9600 • Fax: 703-575-5400
Website: www.ascd.org • E-mail: member@ascd.org
Author guidelines: www.ascd.org/write

Deborah S. Delisle, *Executive Director;* Stefani Roth, *Publisher;* Genny Ostertag, *Director, Content Acquisitions;* Allison Scott, *Acquisitions Editor;* Julie Houtz, *Director, Book Editing & Production;* Miriam Calderone, *Editor;* Melissa Johnston, *Graphic Designer;* Mike Kalyan, *Director, Production Services;* Barton Matheson Willse & Worthington, *Typesetter;* Andrea Hoffman, *Senior Production Specialist*

All web links in this book are correct as of the publication date below but may have become inactive or otherwise modified since that time. If you notice a deactivated or changed link, please e-mail books@ascd.org with the words "Link Update" in the subject line. In your message, please specify the web link, the book title, and the page number on which the link appears.

PAPERBACK ISBN: 978-1-4166-2581-0   ASCD product #118018
PDF E-BOOK ISBN: 978-1-4166-2583-4; see Books in Print for other formats.
Quantity discounts are available: e-mail programteam@ascd.org or call 800-933-2723, ext. 5773, or 703-575-5773. For desk copies, go to www.ascd.org/deskcopy.

ASCD Member Book No. FY18-6A (Apr. 2018 PSI+). ASCD Member Books mail to Premium (P), Select (S), and Institutional Plus (I+) members on this schedule: Jan, PSI+; Feb, P; Apr, PSI+; May, P; Jul, PSI+; Aug, P; Sep, PSI+; Nov, PSI+; Dec, P. For current details on membership, see www.ascd.org/membership.

Library of Congress Cataloging-in-Publication Data

Names: Curwin, Richard L., 1944– author. | Mendler, Allen N., author. | Mendler, Brian D., author.
Title: Discipline with dignity : how to build responsibility, relationships, and respect in your classroom / Richard L. Curwin, Allen N. Mendler, and Brian D. Mendler.
Description: Fourth edition. | Alexandria, Virginia : ASCD, 2018. | Includes bibliographical references and index.
Identifiers: LCCN 2017057169 (print) | LCCN 2017059531 (ebook) | ISBN 9781416625834 (PDF) | ISBN 9781416625810 (pbk.)
Subjects: LCSH: School discipline—United States. | Problem children—Education—United States.
Classification: LCC LB3012.2 (ebook) | LCC LB3012.2 .C87 2018 (print) | DDC 371.5—dc23
LC record available at https://lccn.loc.gov/2017057169

27 26 25 24 23 22 21 20 19 18   1 2 3 4 5 6 7 8 9 10 11 12

↑ To my sister Joyce, who, from the time I was born, has been an inspiration to me. She introduced me to the arts and literature at an early age. More than anything, she showed me the majesty of life.

—RICK CURWIN

↑ To my wife and life partner, Barbara Mendler, for your patience and support during what has been a challenging and emotionally laden process. We got through it, bruised but stronger together than ever. I am forever grateful for all you are in my life.

To my three adult children, Jason, Brian, and Lisa, and their spouses, Ticia, Renee, and Zach, for your love and the gifts of my amazing grandchildren: Caleb, Ava, Megan, Eli, Brookie, and Avi. You enrich my life in ways I have no words to describe.

—ALLEN MENDLER

↑ To Renee: wife, mom, daughter, aunt, and friend. Thank you for the artwork that fills our home. Your talent and passion amaze me every day.

—BRIAN MENDLER

Discipline WITH Dignity

How to Build Responsibility, Relationships, and Respect in Your Classroom

4TH EDITION

Acknowledgments

RICK CURWIN

I would like to thank David Curwin, Andrew Curwin, Menashe Koren, Hagit Furst, Elizabeth Karvonen, Sid Simon, and the students and faculty at David Yellin College.

ALLEN MENDLER

From the depths of my heart and soul, I thank the thousands of educators who have given me the honor of reading my books, attending my seminars, working with me side by side with lots of tough but wonderful students, sharing your strategies with me, and affirming the value of this work by using it to impact the lives of your challenging students in powerful ways. You are too numerous to mention by name, and I would only be doing an injustice to some by trying to list all. You have shown how good discipline is best achieved through relentless respect, shared responsibility, courage to step outside the box, determination, and a never-give-up mentality.

I also want to thank ASCD for many years of supporting our work, culminating in your invitation to do this project, and to Allison, Miriam, and Stefani for your professionalism, kindness, and patience as you guided us along the way.

BRIAN MENDLER

Elijah and Brooklyn, thank you for the joy you provide. I am so grateful I get to be your daddy. I love you both times infinity.

Special thanks to my coauthors, Allen and Rick. This process taught me about loyalty, dedication, friendship, and trust. Congratulations on the 4th edition. I am honored to be a part of it.

To my mom: thanks, sorry, and I love you.

To my brother, sister, sister-in-law, and brother-in-law: thanks, sorry, and I love you.

Jon Crabbe, Elizabeth Sherwood, Diane Long, Colleen Zawadzki, and our staff at the Teacher Learning Center: your expertise, professionalism, and dedication to our business are always appreciated.

Greg Annoni, Beth Schill, Kim Wilks, Kandi Antonetti, Kathleen Skeals, Melissa Stephanski, Tonya Hunskor, Denise Reinert, Charlie Stegall, Lori Charlet, Wendy Claussen, Joseph Corr, Dale Naylor, Laura Glardon, Sylvia Welchans, Penelope Martin-Knox, Yousef Nasouf, Jake Troja, Kristin Dudek, Don Hulin, Dierdre McKinley, and the thousands of other educators that continue to support me: thank you from the bottom of my heart. I wish I could acknowledge you all by name (I really did ask!).

To the What Great Educators Do Differently (#wgedd) crew: Jimmy Casas, Jeff Zoul, Todd Whitaker, Joe Sanfelippo, Kayla Delzer, LaVonna Roth, and everyone else, thanks for inviting me to be a part of such an amazing group. I am honored.

Baruti Kafele: you inspire so many. Thanks for the mentorship. I appreciate you.

To all my social media followers and friends: this career would not be possible without the knowledge and inspiration you give me every day. I am grateful for each of you.

To everyone at Developmental Resources, especially Phil Price and Keli Wickersham: I am thankful and humbled to be such a major part of your conference every year.

Finally, to all the members of my recovery meetings: without you, none of this is possible. "Keep coming back; it works if you work it and you're worth it so work it."

Introduction:
What Is Discipline with Dignity?

When the first edition of *Discipline with Dignity* was published in the 1980s, the United States was in the mood for a strong stand on law and order. Years earlier, protests against the lack of civil rights for minorities and the unequal treatment of women had begun wholesale questioning of and frequent challenges to the status quo. Many people began to view the standards and norms that had defined our institutions for generations as flawed, unfair, and discriminatory.

Schools were not exempt from challenges to the country's values, mores, and practices. Educators were increasingly faced with students who did not behave and parents who were absent, preoccupied, or inclined to side with their children. This situation led to teacher frustration along with demands for more obedience from students and harsher penalties for those who broke the rules. Schools claimed it was easier and fairer to students who worked hard to rid classrooms of students who proved they didn't belong. Programs developed to put control back in the hands of teachers too often relied on rewards and punishments and reduced choices, and they often led to the removal of students who refused to comply. Minorities were affected—and punished—the most. Standardized tests were beginning to be used, not just to judge students but to judge teachers and schools as well. Although these programs seldom work as intended, many schools continue to use them.

Schools became a two-tiered system, with students who followed the rules being rewarded and those who didn't being punished. What educators even now sometimes forget is that removing trouble-makers from school does not eliminate them from life. Young adults who don't graduate from high school cost our society a fortune in expenses related to prison, welfare, and crime. Crime is one job that accepts anyone, regardless of educational status.

We created Discipline with Dignity—an approach that supports various interventions, strategies, and constructs intended to help children make better choices and to make life better for teachers—to offer educators a different vision. When we began, improving student behavior by building relationships was a new concept. Today this approach is much more common, but traditional humiliation, deten-tion, in-school suspension, and suspension remain options in almost all schools we visit; most continue with honor roll and awards assem-blies based solely on grade point average. At the time, we believed that rewards and punishments created winners and losers and did not bring out the best in all students. We realized that many troubled students would not accept simply doing as they were told and would be more likely to comply if they were included in the decisions that affect their lives. We advocated for involving them in developing school and classroom rules and consequences rather than imposing rewards and punishments upon them.

We saw that teachers were no longer being effective using simple obedience methods; we knew that to influence change, teachers needed to earn the trust of their students. We noticed that for some older students, acting out was a choice, done out of disdain for indi-vidual teachers. We watched kids behave perfectly for one teacher and completely disrupt the classroom for a different teacher the next period. We advocated for schools to focus more on creating respon-sible citizens who could think and decide for themselves. We believed humiliating people to gain compliance only sprouted more anger and, ultimately, less compliance. Our vision led to appropriate behavior in the presence and *absence* of authority.

We discovered how much teacher and student stress was a major factor contributing to student misbehavior, so we included what are now called "mindfulness" activities for teachers and students to engage in when upset. We wanted to meet the needs of every student, and although we knew that goal might not always be possible, we wanted every teacher to understand and have strategies to address the unfulfilled needs that lead to inappropriate behavior. We watched and continue to watch teachers have the most success with challenging students by listening closely and then listening more. They ask questions and follow-up questions when things don't seem right. They get to know their students, and they let students get to know them. They relentlessly teach and practice alternative actions students can take when feeling the sadness, anger, frustration, and annoyance that are often at the root of a behavior problem. They are tougher at not giving up than some students are at pushing them away.

Discipline with Dignity is actually an aspirational vision of what schools ought to be. It is highly structured, yet flexible. We designed our approach to help every educator, regardless of philosophy, strengths, and style. Our goal is to produce more responsible students and an easier, more comfortable life for teachers.

Since the publication of the first edition, we continue to learn new and improved ways to positively influence student behavior in a constantly changing world. We have discovered many things about our vision in the last 30 years. The most important is that relationships between teachers and students matter more than rules and consequences for changing behavior. Real change occurs more from informal interventions than from a formal process, and in this edition we emphasize what those interventions are and how to use them. We know that every child can succeed and will behave when the emphasis is more on effort than achievement. After all, no student can do more than try to do his best. There has always been a strong link between discipline and motivation, but most educators need to know specific ways to awaken motivation in today's "difficult" students without resorting to rewards and punishments. This edition explores how to do that.

We are very pleased that previous editions of *Discipline with Dignity* have guided and helped many educators achieve success, especially with students who in times past might have been "thrown away." Yet there remain too many unfulfilled students whose misguided attempts to satisfy their own needs can make life miserable for teachers and peers.

In this new anniversary edition, we continue to build on the themes so many educators found helpful by offering new concepts, strategies, and examples with the same original vision: All students matter and deserve to be treated in a respectful way, even when they misbehave. All teachers deserve a fulfilling career and need an effective structure and strategies when interacting with misbehaving students in order to attain it. *Discipline with Dignity* provides pathways to those outcomes.

Core Beliefs and Principles

Managing student behavior is not easy. It requires a delicate balance between meeting the needs of the group by maintaining social order and meeting the unique needs of each student. Few choices work for all teachers and all students. We believe the best decisions for managing student behavior are based on a value system that maintains the dignity of each student in all situations. We value responsibility more than obedience. Encouraging responsible behavior requires valuing what students think, seeking their input, and teaching them how to make good decisions. We know behavior change is slow, and it occurs in small increments. The expectation that students will change long-standing habits on demand is part of the problem. We advocate a discipline model that is highly structured yet extremely flexible—like a parent who sets clear, firm limits but also provides choice within those limits. We believe discipline should focus on teaching and learning rather than retribution or punishment. Students are the consumers of education, and school should prepare them to flourish and be responsible in choosing their own life destiny.

Core Beliefs Underlying Discipline with Dignity

Discipline is an important part of the job, and every educator must be prepared to accept that reality. We define *discipline* as the process of learning how to get along with others, to solve problems, and to make responsible choices. We believe learning and developing these skills is as important as learning content. Good manners and proper social skills continue to stand the test of time. Content changes. How many planets are in our solar system? Is drinking a glass of wine every night good for you? Answers to these questions continue to change. The value of solving problems without hurting others has been stable for centuries. Although classroom teachers are rarely the primary cause of poor behavior, they must understand that they will not find a lasting solution without owning their role in every successful and unsuccessful situation. Discipline needs to be viewed as a continuous, daily part of the job. We should not get angry with students for not achieving desired results. Instead, we need to stabilize our feelings about the situation and figure out exactly what to do differently next time.

Students always deserve to be treated with dignity. In school, we must let students know that our goal is to always maintain their dignity. Doing so increases trust, builds relationships, and makes problems easier to solve. Treating students with dignity means we stay calm when things around us get crazy. It means we talk to students as privately as possible. It means that even when they are rude, nasty, defiant, and disruptive, we are empathetic, compassionate, and caring. Treating students with dignity means that students see their leader model the behaviors we want them to exhibit. Picture yourself at the receiving end of a discipline method to assess its impact on dignity. Can you imagine how it would feel to be scolded by an administrator at a faculty meeting or in front of your class?

School is for all students, not just the good ones. One of us once taught a class of severely behaviorally disturbed students. Frequently, other teachers asked if they could put some of their regular education students in that class. These teachers believed that if certain students were removed, the class would run much more smoothly. They might have been correct. But school is for every student who attends, not just those we want. The most troubled often need us most. If we choose to think about the situation in a different way, the best students will rarely make us better teachers. It's the ones who create difficulty that force us to expand our skills, and that makes teachers better for all students.

Embracing the journey makes the ride easier. Recently, the fully potty-trained 4-year-old son of one of us pooped in his pants. In the bathroom, Dad was frustrated and said, "Eli, you are 4 years old. It is not OK to go in your pants. You have to feel the pressure on your stomach and go right to the bathroom." If you've ever tried explaining to a 4-year-old what having to go potty feels like, you know it's not easy. A split second later, Dad had a strange experience. He felt like he was watching the interaction between himself and his boy rather than being *in* it. The thought expressed by his many friends and family members who have older children resonated: " 'Embrace it,' " they say. "Sometimes they even grab my shoulders and look me squarely in the eyes while imploring me to 'enjoy the journey. Embrace them being young right now because in a blink they are teenagers.' " Looking back at his son, who now had a tear running down his cheek, Dad's tone turned tender: "It's OK, buddy. We all make mistakes. It's fine. I promise." A moment later, the child's chin was tucked under Dad's neck as they changed his clothes. In this small experience, a (literally) crappy moment was turned into a special interaction that will never be forgotten.

Each of us has the ability to control the attitude we take to each situation and the effort we put into it. Do you embrace the journey of being a teacher, or do you allow every challenging behavior to ruin your day? Mental toughness is a very important component in working with tough students. It is not always easy, but if we are able to embrace the journey, we can enjoy the ride.

Effective discipline often requires courage and creativity. Being effective with difficult students requires a willingness to step outside our comfort zone and respond in unconventional ways. We must be open to approaches that may seem puzzling at first. For example, if you have done everything you can think of to stop a certain behavior but it continues, think of creative ways to legitimize it. If abusive language persists, ask the student to publicly define the offensive words to ensure understanding. If your students like to complain about one thing or another, have a gripe session or a suggestion box in which students are encouraged to deposit complaints that you will read later. If chronic disruptions during study hall are a problem in your school, offer a game-filled, nonacademic study hall or one that focuses on teaching social skills or job-interviewing skills in addition to one that is quiet for those who really want to study.

When misbehavior is legitimized within boundaries, the fun of acting out often fizzles. If a student escalates negative behavior to get himself removed from class, realize that removal simply reinforces negative behavior. He wants out. Instead, send him to the office for doing something good. In this way, visiting the office is a positive experience, and the administrator hears something pleasant.

Good discipline requires short-term solutions without sacrificing long-term goals. Until a misbehaving student changes because his needs are fulfilled, most strategies will only work in the short term. In the last example, a student might test for a day or two by acting appropriately to see if that gets him what he wants. If it does, he may continue to respond but rarely for very long. Unless the content is so stimulating that he *wants* to come to class, more solutions are needed. The goal is identifying the unfulfilled needs causing the behavior and then addressing these regularly through both the curriculum and interactions with the student.

Effective discipline has its own DNA. Good discipline triggers reflection and insight. It is not an action that results solely in pain or pleasure. Chaim Peri, author of *Teenagers Educated the Village Way* (2011), speaks of meaningful punishment as a process of discussion, negotiation, and agreement (DNA). For example, here are two ways to promote an apology. Consider which is more likely to foster empathy and insight:

1. "Matthew, that was a nasty, inappropriate, hurtful thing to say. Apologize to Briana right now, and I don't want to hear that again! Move your card to yellow right now" (or some other punishment).

2. "Matthew, how do you feel when someone says nasty, hurtful things to you? What would you want that person to say or do that might make you feel better? I would feel upset, sad, and maybe mad, and would want someone to apologize and really mean it. However, if you don't sincerely feel sorry, please think of a different way to make things better. What do you think?"

Real change often means sitting with a youngster who breaks rules to have a discussion. Such a discussion makes clear how the behavior is problematic for us, the others involved, or the student. It also affords the student an opportunity to explore other ways of getting his needs met. In the second example involving Matthew, we ask him to put himself at the receiving end of what he did with the goal of helping him repair the harm he caused. We encourage but do not force the apology because we want him to do the right thing without being coerced. As soon as he takes acceptable action, we privately and passionately show our appreciation for him doing the right thing. This approach lets students see the educator as someone who sets limits with others while allowing limits to be set for him- or herself as well. Doing so encourages input from and possible negotiation with the student, promoting responsibility.

Starting fresh every day keeps optimism intact. Great athletes are often noted for having short memories. The faster a quarterback forgets an interception, the better he plays. It's also advisable to have a short memory when working with difficult students. Like primarily looking through a car's windshield to see ahead while periodically checking the rear-view mirrors to stay aware of what's behind, what happened yesterday can be informative but cannot be changed. Look forward. Leave resentments and grudges at the door. You will find strategies in Chapter 9 (on managing stress) that can help you work through whatever troublesome feelings remain. If need be, acknowledge the past ("I know yesterday was tough for both of us, and I want to apologize for saying [or doing] _____."). End by looking out the windshield ("Let's talk about what we can do to make today great."). Although we may not always achieve success and improvement, we must believe that they are always possible. Each student deserves a fresh start fueled by enthusiasm, optimism, and persistence.

Basic Principles of Discipline with Dignity

Let students know what you need, and ask what they need from you. Explain to your class the kind of teacher you are and why. If you are very strict, explain what happened in your life that made you this way. For example, you might say, "In this class I will require you to walk in a straight line and raise your hand before speaking. When I was a child, I was so disorganized that now I am a lunatic in the other direction. Now you know why I care so much about walking in a straight line or raising hands." Ask students how they feel about what you told them. Many teachers do the telling part. Not as many do the asking.

Differentiate instruction based on individual strengths. When a student acts out, the behavior is often a defense against feeling like a failure. If you are unable (or unwilling) to adapt your teaching style to different academic levels based on student ability, do not be surprised when students are disruptive. Teacher expectations that are too high often lead to frustration; those that are too low often lead to students being bored and feeling that success is cheap and not worth the effort. When we make learning too easy, students find little value in it and take little pride in their achievements. Try increasing the challenge without increasing the tedium. For example, if 6th graders are required to master necessary elements in writing a story but one student doesn't understand the difference between a subject and a verb, neither writing a paragraph that contains an example of foreshadowing (a task that is too advanced and frustrating) nor practicing the ABCs (a task that is too easy and boring) is appropriate.

Listen to your students' thoughts and feelings. Active listening potentially defuses troublesome situations. For example, when Denise says, "Mrs. Lewis, this lesson is soooo boring. I hate it," an impulsive response is "If you paid more attention and worked harder, maybe you'd feel differently." Instead say, "I hear you, and I am sorry you feel that way. Can you please tell me two things I can do to help make it better? Thanks for waiting until after class to discuss."

Use humor. Teachers are not paid to be comedians, equipped with an arsenal of jokes. But many frustrating situations can be lightened by poking fun at ourselves and avoiding defensiveness. Make sure students are not the object of any jokes. Frank, a 10th grade student obviously intent on hooking Ms. Johnson into a power struggle, announced in front of the whole class, "You are an asshole!" Keeping a straight face, Ms. Johnson responded by saying, "If you think about it, Frank, that's one body part we all have in common." The class laughed, and a tense moment was quickly defused. It is best to give a consequence or otherwise more fully explore what to do at a time that does not interfere with classroom instruction. To encourage long-term change, it is critical to understand why Frank finds it OK to talk to a teacher this way, and to know what it was that may have contributed to his outburst. (We explore these concerns in more depth throughout the book.)

Vary your style of presentation. Our observations have shown us that most older children have a maximum attention span of 15 minutes and younger children 10 minutes for any one style of presentation. After a 15-minute lecture, it may be a good idea to have a discussion for the next interval. After a large-group discussion, we could switch to small groups. Continually using the same approach creates inattentiveness and restlessness that often lead to disruption.

Offer choices. Teachers and administrators should provide as many opportunities as possible for children to make decisions. It's better to set limits before offering choice. Here are some examples:

> "Sitting here doing nothing during silent reading is not OK. You can choose any book from the library to read. Do you need suggestions?"

> "Keeping your head down in class is not OK because it distracts me and I worry about you. If I see that happening today, will it be better if I tap you on the shoulder, whisper in your ear or [jokingly] pretend to be a waterfall?"

> "When people call you names, tell them you don't like it, walk away, or ask me for a suggestion."

Encouraging students to make decisions and then live with the outcome of those decisions teaches responsibility. The most effective discipline is done *with* students rather than *to* them.

Use a variety of ways to communicate with students. In addition to the spoken word, caring gestures and nonverbal messages are effective. Some students do better when they get feedback on a sticky note, in an e-mail, or on the phone. It is important to keep in mind that reports of inappropriate relationships between teachers and students are extremely unsettling and dangerous. Awareness of sexual harassment and abuse is growing day by day. Touching must never cross a professional line. Although touch can be a very effective way to communicate caring, we understand that many educators have become wary of false accusations. Certainly, we need to be respectful of physical boundaries and use common sense. However, a pat on the back, a touch on the shoulder, a handshake, or a high-five can help form bonds with many tough-to-reach children.

Recognize that being fair does not always mean treating students equally. Systems and plans are a necessary part of teaching. They guide us so we don't have to make first-time decisions whenever something happens that is new to us. On the one hand, by predetermining consequences, we reduce the need for thinking, save time, and can blame the system if the action is ineffective. On the other hand, if we rely too much on the system, we may fail to do what is best for each individual. A system that narrowly interprets behavior ends up treating all students the same. These systems fail when a more individualized approach is required. The best systems give teachers and students choices for how to solve problems so the best solution is used. They balance predictability and flexibility. They can be fair but not always equal. Once students and parents understand the difference between "fair" and "equal," we can differentiate behavior-control methods just as we differentiate instructional strategies. You will find much more on this topic in Chapter 6, where we talk about consequences.

2

Out-of-School and In-School Causes of Discipline Problems

Jon, a student growing up in foster care, summed up his situation:

> I do not have parents. I mean, not a mom and a dad the way you would think of it. I live in a foster home, which means I go home every night to paid employees. These people have their own children they take to Disney World. Nobody takes me. They act happy when I get a good grade or have a good report card, but it's not like [what] my friends get to experience when they get home! Holidays and breaks are a disaster. I do not go on vacation. I sit home thinking about where my real mom is, why she left me, and if I'll ever see her again. Honestly, your English homework is the farthest thing from my mind right now.

Jon is not alone, and success for children like him is rare. According to Christian (2003), educational deficits of foster children are reflected in more retention in grade, lower test scores, and higher rates of absenteeism, tardiness, truancy, and dropping out. Their poor academic performance affects their lives after foster care, contributing to higher-than-average rates of homelessness, criminality, drug abuse, and unemployment.

Out-of-School Causes

Foster care is just one of many out-of-school issues that affect in-school behavior. In the third edition of this book, we identified the most common outside influences on behavior, including such factors as family life, poverty, and diminished social civility. In the 10 years since that edition was published, these causes are still relevant. However, with the explosion of technology, some new out-of-school causes have developed. In this section we discuss the most prominent causes—both long-standing and more recently noticeable.

Dysfunctional Families

Some children go home to dysfunctional biological families. In these homes, many basic values and behaviors are not taught. Words like *please, thank you,* and *share* are not spoken, so children do not learn appropriate ways to use them. In some families, the values necessary for success at school are either untaught or unlived. In such cases, good discipline is about educators taking time to teach skills that parents might typically teach.

Good discipline is also about understanding. Imagine two people with bad headaches. A physician determines that the first person's headaches are caused by eyestrain. The patient gets glasses and the headache goes away. The second person has a brain tumor and needs immediate surgery. Both people have the same symptom (headaches). By understanding why the headaches exist, each is properly treated. Similarly, by understanding the causes of behavior problems, we are able to work around them. Start by asking the student. Press beyond responses like "I don't know" and "He did it first." For example, in a calm moment after being called an offensive name, you might say, "I do not like being called a bitch, and talking that way is not OK. I am sorry you got so upset. Please explain what made you so angry." After listening to the student's response, teach and practice alternate ways to handle the emotion. Here's one possibility:

So calling names only makes the problem worse. The problem is anger and frustration. Calling names is the symptom of the problem.

For the rest of your life you will feel anger and frustration from time to time. Close your eyes and picture the person you are angry at. On the count of three, punch the person in the face with your breath instead of your hands. When we use our breath, nobody gets hurt and there are no consequences.

Children are often exposed to violence and become desensitized to it after a while. When children see abuse, they often abuse others. When they hear bad language, it becomes the way they talk.

Trauma

Trauma occurs in many forms, including physical, sexual, or verbal abuse; violence; neurological trauma caused by exposure to toxins such as lead; homelessness; and poor nutrition. The more adverse experiences children are exposed to, the more difficult it is for them to overcome the effects of the trauma. Traumatized children often have an underdeveloped frontal cortex—the area where the brain does its high-level decision making—and an overdeveloped fight-or-flight reflex. That combination can make it extremely difficult to stay composed when stressed and on-task in class, leading to higher suspension and dropout rates, which in turn often lead to decreased life expectancy and a greater likelihood of incarceration.

Social Media

Social media, although beneficial in making information available to all and creating a democracy of knowledge, also contains forums where anonymous shaming of children, increased access to sexual predators, and sexting have proliferated. A principal we worked with estimates that 80 percent of student-on-student problems begin online. Snapchat, Instagram, Facebook, and Twitter are just a few platforms that many students access frequently. With technology changing so quickly, these platforms are likely to be replaced by others within the next few years.

We tell students two specific things about social media. First, a post is like toothpaste squirted from the tube: once out, it is impossible to put back. Even if you delete a message, someone might have shared or forwarded it. Second, if you have to think about posting a message or photo, *don't*. If you hesitate even a moment because of fear that you might offend or humiliate another person or yourself, don't hit "Send." Bullying online via social media has become too widespread and dangerous to ignore; a single tweet can reach thousands of others in seconds. So, while recognizing that social media is not going away and can also be used for good, we advocate that schools require instruction in the appropriate use of social media.

Diminished Social Civility

When political and civic leaders cannot discuss issues without blaming, calling each other names, and painting their opponents as evil, is it surprising that children see name-calling and put-downs as acceptable methods of communication? What was once respectful disagreement expressed through civil discourse has turned into baseless insults and accusations hurled by politicians and media "analysts." This kind of behavior has become normalized over the years, leading to political divides and a loss of respect for others.

Some forms of music and popular culture are also problematic. When song lyrics including hateful and unacceptable words like *nigger, faggot, wetback, kike,* and *ho* are considered OK as long as you belong to a certain ethnic group, the boundaries of civility and decency have been ruptured. Television shows and electronic media are often overly graphic, displaying bloody scenes, inappropriate language, and what some might consider soft pornography. Comedy is often a series of insults punctuated with foul language, sexual innuendo, and adults looking stupid. Even the news often features a proliferation of uncensored violent acts. These pervasive images negatively affect the way students talk, how they interact socially, and the respect they show teachers, making discipline far more difficult.

Political Correctness Run Amok

Individually, we (the authors) have fought racism, from the civil rights battles in the 1960s to working in majority-minority schools to help improve education for those who face racially based difficulties. We do not tolerate stereotyping or racism of any kind. But we believe that political correctness has run amok. For example, the *New York Times* reported that students at Oberlin College in Ohio protested the serving of inauthentic Chinese food in the dining hall on grounds that it constituted racism (Rogers, 2015). Speakers with controversial views have been shouted offstage or disinvited from speaking on college campuses. Although sensitivity to others' feelings is a wonderful development, sometimes it goes too far. Not surprisingly, a backlash to political correctness has developed. Many people say offensive things that are "unacceptable" with the intent of countering political correctness. Children are caught in the crossfire, some overly sensitive and others overly offensive.

A Sense of Entitlement

An informal study found that children nag their parents nine times on average before getting what they want. Some youth sports leagues award players trophies just for showing up. The result of these kinds of behavior is a selfish attitude. Unwittingly, many schools reinforce this sense of entitlement through the proliferation of rewards and bribe systems in which stickers, stars, and points become substitutes for doing the right thing simply because it is the right thing to do. Children are taught that what they have is more important than who they are or what they do.

With the push of a button, we can communicate with anyone anywhere in the world. We can download hundreds of songs in seconds, be entertained nonstop by devices that start and stop by voice command, and enter a virtual world doing almost anything instantly with amazing graphics. Given the lightning speed of development, leading to ever newer and quicker breakthroughs, even these technologies are likely to be yesterday's news by the time you read this book.

When students realize that grades at school aren't given but *earned,* and timely thought and study are usually required to master a concept, some become frustrated and angry at the audacity of an "unfair" teacher trying to hold them accountable in a world for which they are poorly prepared.

A College-Track Economy

Despite current concerns voiced by many parents about the affordability of college, it is important to realize that it is difficult to get a job that pays the bills without at least a college degree *or* training in a skilled trade. According to the Bureau of Labor Statistics (2016), a high school graduate's median salary in 2016 was $35,256, compared with $59,124 for a college graduate. High school dropouts can expect to earn $10,000 less than graduates. At the same time, however, we must realize that college is not for everyone. According to salary.com, the average pay for a plumber is $49,000 per year, and electricians make close to $58,000. These are well-paying jobs that will always be needed. We do a disservice to students when we do not introduce them to the option of pursuing a skilled trade. High school students who aren't successful in traditional classes or have lost interest in achieving academic success are better directed to pursue training that is compatible with their abilities and interests and may also lead to a well-paying and fulfilling career. Otherwise, feelings of hopelessness, anger, and fear of the future may lead them to disruptive classroom behavior.

Lack of a Secure Family Environment

Perhaps the greatest influence on children is the quality of their home life. Society continues to undergo major shifts in values and traditions. Single-parent families, families with two working parents, two-mommy or two-daddy families, and blended families exist in just about every community. Amid constantly shifting family patterns, a discipline problem is often symptomatic of a child's anxiety and insecurity. In 1970, 12 percent of children were born to unwed mothers, compared to more than 40 percent in 2015 (Martin, Hamilton, Osterman, Driscoll, & Mathews, 2017, p. 8). The U.S. divorce rate has risen steadily—so much so that some states have more divorces than marriages. Children of divorced parents generally perform worse than their peers in most academic settings (Crow & Ward-Lonergan, 2003; Potter, 2010). Although divorce is not necessarily a predictor of problems at school, children with divorced parents are more likely to struggle with issues of emotional security than their classmates from more stable families. Knowing about a child's family relationships can be helpful in making adjustments at school. Look for patterns. We recall Christina, who went to her dad's house on Tuesdays. He was a nice guy but much less structured than Christina's mom. Christina was often exhausted on Wednesday. Knowing this, her teacher would say, "I know it is Wednesday morning and on Tuesday nights you go to your dad's house. Was everything good there last night? What did you do? Did you get along with everyone, including his new girlfriend? Did you sleep? If not, how about I give you 10 minutes, and then you give me 10 minutes of work?" In other words, this teacher knew to plan for Wednesdays being a challenge for Christina.

Concentration of Poverty

Numerous studies over many years have shown a strong correlation between socioeconomic status (SES) and success in school. Generally speaking, students from wealthier families do significantly better than those from poorer families. We are not talking about the values of poor parents; in nearly every community across the United States, parents seek the best schools for their children. In their aspirations to provide a "better" life for their families, many low-SES parents must work two or three jobs or learn a new language, factors that make it more difficult for them to support their children's school experience on an everyday basis. Their children, like all children, need and deserve access to the best educational resources. Yet the schools with the best reputations are almost always in upper-middle-class suburban neighborhoods with a preponderance of white children.

The "best schools," including those in impoverished neighborhoods, have a culture among students where it is cool to be successful. In too many poorly performing schools, achievement is considered to be uncool or a sign of selling out. Top students often feel like they need to hide being smart. To counteract this tendency, try to create a classroom culture where doing well is cool. One way to do this is by rewarding everyone in the class in honor of one person's success. "Because I am so proud of Anthony, everyone gets an extra 20 minutes on the playground in honor of him."

On a visit with 11-year-old Victor—one of the authors' "little brothers" in the Big Brothers Big Sisters program—Victor spontaneously said that he would never want to go away to college because he wouldn't want to leave his family. When this very bright boy was asked if he knew anyone in his neighborhood who was going to college, Victor could not think of a single person. He is one of many who face an uphill struggle to success because he has no community context for how education can really improve life. A recent discussion with a friend of one of the authors makes a similar point. The friend, who lives in a small enclave of beautifully maintained homes within an otherwise decaying city, matter-of-factly noted that all the young families move out as soon as their children reach school age because they do not want to send their children to an urban school.

In the last edition of this book, published in 2008, we suggested that radical solutions to this problem may be necessary. Since then, to increase the economic diversity of their student populations, more than 80 school districts reportedly consider socioeconomic status in student assignment, with results showing increased achievement among low-SES students when compared with similar students in less diverse schools (Potter, 2013). Perhaps the time has come to more broadly use socioeconomic status to define school enrollment. The reported data do not identify the actual percentage of low-SES students attending these diverse schools. Until such data are available, we would ideally like to see how low-SES students perform in schools where no more that 20 percent of the population qualifies for free-and-reduced lunch. Although we recognize the logistical and political problems that would likely arise from such an effort, our speculation is that low-SES students in such schools would show considerable academic growth.

Although there are few quick-fix solutions to the factors cited here, an impressive base of research begun long ago strongly suggests that a caring, mentoring relationship plays a huge role in contributing to resiliency of at-risk youth (Ellis, Small-McGinley, & De Fabrizio, 1999; Werner & Smith, 1989). Developing such relationships requires talking with students about things other than content. Get to know students on a personal level. Ask questions. If they do not answer, tell them about yourself. Educators get daily opportunities to offer students nurturance that can dramatically affect student behavior and sometimes change lives. And remember that relationships can take months to build and seconds to ruin.

Gangs and Drugs

Gangs and drugs have been societal problems for many decades. However, the recent escalation of both, and their unholy connection, continues to affect school children at younger ages. Until recently, opioid pain medications were very easy to obtain legally. Two problems have emerged from this phenomenon. First, more people have become addicted to these drugs, and when their prescriptions expire, they may seek lower-cost heroin as an alternative, resulting in a new group of heroin addicts. Second, prescription drugs have high monetary value on the street, creating new income streams for dealers.

The demand for these drugs has given gangs more money, which they can then use to buy advanced military weaponry. The result is more teenagers being killed by gang violence in communities throughout the nation, Chicago being just one example. An article in the *Chicago Tribune* stated, "A closer look at the numbers shows the intractable hold that violence has in some of Chicago's 22 police districts" (Sweeney & Gorner, 2016). A complex mix of factors drives the violence. But experts say that much of the bloodshed can be linked to gang conflict over everything from petty disputes to control of drug dealing, as well as the splintering of gangs into smaller cliques fighting over a few blocks at a time, with easy access to guns.

In-School Causes

Out-of-school causes of discipline problems are often well beyond the capacity of educators to fix. We can empathize and—within the confines of a school day—offer as much emotional support as possible. Fortunately, we have many more opportunities to address in-school factors, which mix with out-of-school issues to cause or exacerbate discipline problems. Because educators have much more control over what goes on inside school, these causes will be discussed throughout

the book in much more detail, along with strategies that can effectively address them.

Test-Driven Environment

The pressure of testing continues to preoccupy both teachers and
students. Teachers are expected to cover so much material they sometimes forget that it doesn't matter what they teach if students don't
learn it. Teachers are not to blame. Test scores often help determine
a school's resources, state aid, and staffing. Resolving conflicts with
students and teaching them ways to act more appropriately have taken
a back seat to test-related pressures. The focus on test scores can create an environment where the student is far more likely to be considered a *product* of education than a *consumer*.

Competitive Environment

Many schools remain highly competitive environments where
students compete for recognition, grades, and spots on sports teams.
We believe academic competition is different from real-life competition. In life, people get a chance to compete in a field, a profession, or
an industry they choose. If unsuccessful, they can switch. In school,
on the other hand, we drop all 7-year-olds in 2nd grade and force
them to compete. When some do not succeed, we label them problem
students. Competition is fine when playing football or basketball or
trying out for the school musical. We love competition when chosen
but do not like it when forced.

With regard to academic achievement and behavioral improvement, replace competition *between students* with competition *within
each student*. Evaluate students' performance and offer assignments
based on getting each student to be better today than he was yesterday.
Focus on improvement! If a student shows lesser performance than
her capability would suggest is possible, challenge her to do better even
if her initial performance is best in the class. Although honor rolls are
institutional fixtures at most schools, we believe their elimination
would make schools better places. But most schools are unwilling to
let go of this tradition, so it might be more feasible to consider having
"on-a-roll" in your classes, with a focus only on improvement. Say, for

example, that last week Jenny scored 40 percent on her spelling test. This week her score was 62 percent. Traditional scoring calls her performance on both tests a failure. Yet she improved by 50 percent in one week! Unless improvement is acknowledged, many students will eventually give up. Privately, at the end of the day, give Jenny a certificate of improvement to take home.

Scripted Curriculum

Classroom curriculum is often predetermined by individuals far removed from the classroom, with little and sometimes no deviation allowed. All academic classes must cover the exact same material regardless of students' ability and needs. Teachers lack the ability or permission to individualize, which creates grave problems for students who have no place on the curriculum map. This situation is exasperating for good teachers who realize that reaching challenging students requires showing how the content is relevant to their lives. Without flexibility to create curriculum and materials, many teachers feel locked into teaching material they know doesn't connect with their students. The result is students often failing to see how school is relevant. Teachers as well as students are frustrated by this approach, which leads to conflict between the two.

Student Boredom

Some students sit up straight, appear attentive by making eye contact, nod their heads every so often, and present themselves as interested and somewhat involved, even when bored. Others show zero desire to hide boredom. They withdraw—head down, hood up, and earphones plugged in—and look unmotivated; or they act out, unconcerned with the consequences of poor grades, a trip to the office, or a phone call home.

Powerlessness

All people like to feel some level of power and control in their lives. Some students rebel to voice dissatisfaction with their lack of influence. In most schools, students are told for six hours every day where to go, what time to be there, how long to take for basic biological necessities, which learning is relevant, what to learn, and how their learning will be evaluated. They are told rules, consequences, how to dress, and when to talk. When one group (adults) develops rules and procedures that define behavioral standards for another group (students) that has had little or no input, a conflict of control and power can result. When school is unfulfilling, this lack of power can trigger anger and opposition.

Unclear Limits

Setting limits is important to good discipline and improved behavior. Teachers and administrators should be clear and specific as to which behaviors will and will not be tolerated. In addition, we promote respect for and among students when we explain why limits exist. Although many educators intuitively know this, our busy lives too often preclude spending adequate time addressing this issue.

Requiring Students to Earn Special School Activities

Most schools require that certain appealing activities be earned instead of given. These opportunities include field trips, pizza parties, playground privileges, "Fun Friday," and even staying in the classroom for special time with the teacher. But in many cases, the students who most need these opportunities are the ones who rarely earn them. Because they feel left out, these students tend to denigrate the opportunities denied them by calling the activities "stupid"—or worse. "Good" students get increased opportunities to learn social skills and feel wanted, while "bad" students rarely get the experience needed to improve behavior. Most just feel left out.

Lack of Acceptable Outlets to Express Feelings

One of the authors recalls teaching 11th grade English. Tara walked into class one day threatening to hurt another student. She was asked to write down how she felt and explain why she felt that way. She then had to write a solution to the problem that did not involve violence. We discussed the issue, and it was peacefully resolved. Students and teachers need to have acceptable ways to release emotions, thoughts, and feelings without getting into trouble. A middle school teacher we know in Kansas City keeps an overstuffed "punching" pillow in her room. Any time a student feels angry, pounding the pillow is an option. Find ways for students to express feelings. Listen to *what* students are saying without hearing *how* they are saying it. The "how" often gets in the way of the "what."

Shaming Students Who Are Noncompliant

Shaming consists of publicly embarrassing students to gain compliance. Some shamed students develop resistance to these techniques and their behavior worsens. Others begin to hate school and carry embarrassment well into the future. Confidence decreases and enthusiasm is lost. All public interventions—including writing names on the board and clipping (moving clothespins up and down a public chart as behavior changes)—run the risk of shaming.

Lack of Success

Many students with chronic behavior problems believe they cannot be successful in school. Such students appear to give up before trying. They do not believe they can receive the attention and recognition needed through school achievement. They see themselves as losers and stop trying to gain mainstream acceptance. Their self-message is "Since I can't be recognized as anything other than a failure, I'll protect myself from feeling hurt. To do nothing is better than to try and fail. And to be recognized as a troublemaker is better than being seen as stupid."

Schools Do Make a Difference

Other than home, school is where students spend most of their time. Teachers continue to significantly influence the lives of children. The vast majority of successful teachers care about their students as people first and students second. They show respect by involving students in the decisions that will affect them, challenging them with relevant material that is neither too easy nor too hard, caring about them by showing genuine interest in what they enjoy doing, and both correcting and appreciating them with thoughtfulness and dignity.

3

Threats, Punishments, and Rewards: Why Most Traditional Discipline Methods Don't Work

Most schools identify *responsibility* as a core value, yet many rely exclusively on methods of *obedience* when rules are broken. We define an *obedient* student as one who follows rules without question, regardless of philosophical beliefs, ideas of right and wrong, instincts and experiences, or values. A student "does it" because he is told to do it. The system defines right and wrong. The only choice is to do as told or to not do as told. In the short term, obedience may offer teachers relief, a sense of power and control, and an oasis from the constant bombardment of defiance. In the long run, however, obedience leads to student immaturity, a lack of responsibility, an inability to think critically, and a feeling of helplessness that is manifested by withdrawal, aggressiveness, or power struggles. Obedience is implemented primarily with *threats, punishments,* and *rewards* (bribes).

Threat Versus Choice

Imagine walking down the street and a dangerous-looking person approaches. He puts a gun to your head and says, "Your money or your life." One way to respond might be "I am a teacher. I don't have any money, and I'm not even sure if I have much of a life." Is the statement

"Your money or your life" a choice or a threat? Even though two "choices" are offered, clearly the question is a threat.

The difference matters, because when we're threatened, we begin sweating. Our heartbeat increases and our body temperature rises. Adrenaline and cortisone course through our body. These changes are autonomic, not chosen. They often create a fight-or-flight response. Other responses include freezing in place, immediately complying, or blaming others. Because most attacks on humans are psychological, a student's fight-or-flight response is also psychological. It results in aggression or fear—or both—and is expressed as arguments, temper tantrums, name-calling, withdrawal, and passive-aggressive behavior. Examples of the latter include the silent treatment or the game of "Guess Why I'm Angry." A student will often roll her eyes, whisper behind your back, or collapse with head down and hood up. She will not say what is wrong. Teachers and peers are left guessing what the problem is. Other passive-aggressive behaviors include slamming doors, loudly dropping things, spilling drinks, or covering the ears. When students perceive choices as threats, they react as though they have been asked, "Your money or your life?" They harbor resentment over the fact that we forced an action by threatening them.

Choices are very different from threats. Suppose you have a serious accident and badly hurt your leg. The doctor says, "I can save your life by amputating your leg, or I can try to save your leg, but you might die in surgery. Your choice." In the gun scenario, the person with the gun is in control. In the doctor scenario, the patient has control. This is how we define "true choice." Both scenarios have negative alternatives to select from yet are different because of who has control. Giving students control—even when the choices are unpleasant—is really the key. Do the options presented require actual decision making?

Two questions help determine who has control. The first is this: Is the correct choice already decided before being offered? For example, a teacher says, "If you don't clean up, you will miss recess. The choice is yours." The teacher obviously wants the student to clean up. The correct "choice" is already determined. Adding "the choice is yours" makes no real difference. Instead, the teacher might say, "Thanks for considering cleaning up before recess," which sets a limit and conveys a clear expectation without being threatening; and she might add, "Would you prefer to do it yourself or pick a friend to help?" Notice the teacher has stated no preference; she also thanks the student *before* the clean-up.

The second question for determining control is this: Does the choice offer punishment or something bad if the "wrong" choice is made? Punishment is always part of a threat, even when a choice is offered. Saying "If you say that again, I'll send you to the office" presents a threat. From their perspective, students hear this: "If I don't do what I'm asked/told, I will be hurt in some way." Aggression or fight-or-flight behavior usually follows. Here are some other examples of threats:

- "Do your homework or I'll call your parents."
- "If you say that again, I will take away a ticket."
- "One more incident of name-calling and you are staying after school with me."

All of these are threats because one choice is teacher-preferred and the other is a punishment. Even if the word *choice* is added, the effect is the same. The student does what is demanded because he must in order to avoid punishment, not because he wants to or because he believes it is a better choice.

Sometimes it is hard to tell whether a threat is really a choice. Frequently what the teacher may initially view as a punishment is actually a legitimate choice in the eyes of the student. Some students are content to choose the alternative that the teacher prefers he avoid. For example, "Do your work now or during lunch" can go either way. If the student likes doing work at lunchtime, he will pick that alternative. The teacher must be comfortable with both choices offered.

Sometimes students might not be afraid of the punishment contained in the threat. Teachers are then left with a punishment they prefer not to use and they still fail to get students to comply. If the threat isn't carried out, students learn that sometimes the teacher will back down. Some students learn to use a threat against the teacher. For example, a teacher says, "Chris, either pick up your trash or go to the office." Chris retorts, "OK, I'll go to the office. I hate being here anyway." If you are not prepared for Chris's response, then don't offer the alternative.

Knowing When to Use Threats

When danger and safety are involved, a threat is often the preferred strategy. Threatening to physically grab a student is a really bad idea—unless it is the only way to stop a child from running across a busy street. When danger and safety are involved, immediate results matter most.

If you intend to threaten, know that you are threatening and don't tell yourself that you are offering a choice. Use threats carefully and infrequently. Do not threaten unless you intend to follow through. Sometimes teachers make the threat so scary they are sure it will work; if it doesn't, they need the will to carry it out.

Choices and Limits

We prefer choice to threat because it is respectful and usually much more effective with challenging students. Choice does not mean allowing students to do whatever they want, however. Choices that teach responsibility must have clearly defined limits. The goal is to set boundaries while offering movement (decision making or control) to students who have either too much or too little control in other aspects of their lives. Limits define the parameters of that control. Think of choice as being like a batter's box on a baseball field. The lines defining the box represent limits. Within the box (limits), hitters are allowed to move up or back (choice), depending on the pitcher. Teachers who are oriented toward an authoritarian approach do not usually offer enough choice, whereas indulgent teachers offer too much, with few limits.

Choices and limits go hand in hand when teaching responsibility. Some people think that students in the developed world have too many choices and are unequipped to handle them. Others consider the bigger problem to be too few limits. When the balance is out of alignment on either side, responsibility problems develop. Too few choices can lead to rebellion or dependency, with students not getting opportunities to practice making their own decisions. Too few limits can lead to narcissism, because students may believe they can have whatever they want.

Punishments Versus Consequences/Interventions

Have you ever gotten a speeding ticket? Most of us have. When handed the ticket, did you say to yourself, "Now I'll be a better driver" or "Darn, I should have seen the cop!" After getting the ticket, did you slow down for a couple of hours and watch extra closely for police officers? Did you buy a radar detector? We have asked these questions many times when working with adult groups. The answers from the vast majority of people indicate more remorse for getting a ticket than for speeding. When asked the next question, "Why did you get the ticket?" answers usually include "I was breaking the law"; "Speeding is unsafe"; "The government needs the money"; "I didn't know the speed limit"; and "It's a stupid speed limit, especially at that hour." All these answers and others like them are related to getting a ticket, but none of them hits the nail on the head. The real answer is "I got caught." If we don't get caught, the other reasons are irrelevant.

Getting a speeding ticket teaches us many lessons. The most common is "Don't get caught." Punishing students teaches the same lesson. When discussing with educator groups the "don't get caught" mentality that punishments teach, a common response is "Well, you have to do *something*." Wrong. We have to do the *right* thing. No one wants a doctor who prescribes a knee replacement to cure a broken wrist because the doctor had to do *something*.

The goal of punishment is to control another's behavior. Punishments have four objectives for controlling student behavior:

1.   To inflict pain when a student does something wrong so that he associates pain with that behavior. Therefore, he won't do it again.

2.   To send a message to all students. Deterrence extends beyond the misbehaving student to all the students in the class. When students see their classmates get punished, they fear the same might happen to them.

3.   To give the teacher the ability to control students.

4.   To give the teacher the feeling of being in control, whether or not control is real.

Punishments also offer the false promise of saving time. Because punishments can be done quickly, teachers often prefer them to interventions that require more time. However, if you add up all the time it takes for the class to refocus on the lesson and the number of times you must repeat a punishment over the course of the year, you'll find that punishments are usually a time waster.

Punishments are actions that your students do not want done to them, such as being placed in isolation, scolded, forced to apologize, and humiliated. Punishments also include the removal of something your student likes, such as computer time, recess, and a toy or book. The results of punishment may vary, but one thing remains constant: it reduces student responsibility. Punishment takes control away from students and gives it to the person inflicting the punishment.

The most positive result of punishment is how quickly it works in the short term. When punishment is effective, the behavior change is immediate. Unfortunately, this effect rarely lasts and often leads to long-term problems. An occasional punishment sends the message that certain limits are nonnegotiable because safety is extremely important. When administered in the context of a caring relationship between teacher and student, it can be very effective. However, over time, punishments break trust, and they increase lying and excuse making. Phrases such as "I didn't do it," "She started it," and "It wasn't my fault" are symptomatic of excessive punishment.

Some teachers think punishments are more severe than consequences and teach a more powerful lesson. In reality, we often choose a punishment because it is less dangerous than the harshness of a natural consequence. In fact, punishments are often used to protect people from consequences. Look at the following examples and choose which is harsher, consequence or punishment:

1. Abusing drugs:
   - Possible punishment: Jail
   - Possible consequence: Death
2. Touching a hot stove:
   - Possible punishment: A slap on the hand
   - Possible consequence: A burned hand

Chapter 6 (on formal discipline) includes much more discussion on replacing punishments with effective consequences. In the next sections we discuss some additional forms of punishment that need expanded explanation.

Forced Apologies

We often hear teachers say, "Apologize to your classmate right now!" This approach is not the best solution to a problem between classmates. Asking a student to apologize can explode into a much bigger issue. If a student refuses, it is easy to escalate the request into a demand. If the student gives in, she might associate apologies with a loss of power and control. Future apologies will be less forthcoming. If the student is defiant or we become defiant, a power struggle will result. No matter who prevails, no one really wins. The issue is no longer about remorse; it's about control.

It's not that apologies are bad. In fact, apologizing with genuine remorse is one of the most important social skills we can teach students. Heartfelt apologies can potentially heal many wounds. Students become more responsible when they learn empathy and express regret when they create hurt. It is better to suggest rather than to force an apology. For example, you can say, "Do you think what you did was wrong and deserves an apology? If you are really sorry, it will help to tell Charlie." If the student either doesn't think what she did was wrong or doesn't think an apology is warranted and you disagree, explain your perspective: "I realize you think Charlie started the argument, but apologizing for how you reacted shows how mature you are." If the student still doesn't see it your way, consider a different consequence or intervention.

Students don't learn empathy when their apologies are forced. Hearing a forced apology can anger the person on the receiving end. Have you ever received an insincere apology? How did you feel? How do you feel when a politician or a sports star goes on television and "sincerely" reads an apology? Does your trust in that person go up or down? The other serious problem with forced apologies is that they teach students that they can get away with almost anything as long as they apologize. Do we want students to learn that they can do anything as long as they say "I'm sorry"? It is far better to discuss what it feels like to be hurt or violated and to learn that expressing genuine regret helps the other person feel better.

Taking Away Privileges

Imagine yourself as you were in middle or high school in a class full of other students. Your teacher announces a field trip to one of your favorite places. Everyone is abuzz with excitement. Then she pulls you aside after class and says firmly, "Your behavior has been unacceptable, and so you are not going because I can't trust you."

Would you be more likely to say to yourself or out loud to the teacher, "I really wanted to go on that trip; please let me" or "Who cares? It's a stupid trip. I didn't want to go anyway." If you chose the first option, how many additional lost privileges would it take before you picked the second option? Eventually, taking away privileges erodes the teacher's power because the student stops caring or pretends he doesn't but feels resentful. The student prefers to denigrate the privilege rather than feel badly about it being removed. Once a student regularly thinks this way, he protects himself from hurt and acts like he doesn't care. The best solution is to separate privileges from the discipline process, using these guidelines:

- Don't take away privileges once offered (so be careful what you offer).
- Don't include loss of privileges as a threat.
- Don't arbitrarily include loss of privileges as a punishment.

Collective Punishment

Collective punishment is used to create intense pressure on a group to control individual members. The idea is to punish the entire group for the actions of individuals. Here are some examples:

- In basic training in the army, a sergeant punishes a whole barracks if one soldier makes his bed improperly.

• A government official in a third-world dictatorship burns a village if one of the villagers commits a crime.

And here are some examples of teachers using collective punishment:

• "If Lisa doesn't pick up her things, then we aren't going to watch the video."
• "Because Ricardo didn't do his homework last night, no one can use the computer."

Although the pressure on the individual student to behave is powerful, this technique is riddled with problems. Consider the following three possibilities:

1.   If one student is responsible for the misery of others, a lot of anger, blame, and accusations might follow. The result can be fighting, name-calling, or isolation of the student responsible for the collective punishment. Punishing the entire class because of one student also gives that student way too much power over everyone else.

2.   Giving the inappropriate behavior all of the attention essentially ignores the responsible behavior of everyone else. This does little to promote responsibility and teaches that even those who do the right thing suffer the same outcome as someone who misbehaves.

3.   A student may use collective punishment to get even with her peers for a perceived wrong inflicted on her. In this case, the teacher acts as an agent of punishment for the misbehaving student.

Rewards as Bribes: Weighing the Risks

One of the most common strategies used by teachers to get students to comply is to reward them. Many teachers see rewards as the opposite of punishment and more enjoyable to use, and rewards often produce positive results. However, these assumptions are mostly false. Rewards and punishments have the same goal. They are both methods of controlling student behavior. They teach the opposite of responsibility as we define it.

Rewards are bribes. They are easy, fast, and will often change behavior in the short term. But rarely do these changes last unless the rewards become bigger and better. Rewards can create a sense of entitlement. Bribes usually lead to improved behavior in the presence of authority because students know they will get something. However, our goal is for students to behave when an authority figure is not present.

Deciding whether any strategy works requires an examination of the strategy's benefit and cost. Hundreds of responses to bad behavior might get a preferred result, but teachers would never use them because of the negative consequences (for example, taping a student's mouth shut will stop his talking, but it's an unacceptable approach). Many documented studies have clearly demonstrated that rewards may often change behavior. We do not dispute the idea that rewards can be effective. Our question is this: Are rewards worth the risk?

Let's examine the dangers and potential harm rewards can cause. If you still wish to use a reward with a specific child, you will be able to make a more informed decision than you would by answering this simple question: Do rewards work? To begin, keep in mind that bribes and use of rewards can harm intrinsic motivation, encourage unrealistic expectations, and create dependency. Let's look at each of these concerns.

Harming Intrinsic Motivation

Some parents pay their children for good grades with cash, clothes, or prizes. Some teachers do the same. Certainly, some students' grades might improve with the opportunity to get something favorable, but at what cost? No student ever improves behavior by bribe or reward if he is doing his best already.

There are many definitions of learning, from a change in knowledge to a change in skill to a change in understanding. All definitions include the word *change*. Rewards encourage students to make a change, but only for a short time. How many times have you passed a test that you would likely struggle with a week later? Bribes encourage students to be "finishers" (someone who checks a task off a list) and possibly even cheaters rather than learners. Bribes send the message that desirable behavior is a commodity to be bought and sold.

Further, some students will be unable to meet the requirements even if they give 100 percent to the effort, creating a situation where they feel punished for not doing as told, even though they tried. Research shows that

> Traditional extrinsic rewards work well for motivating workers to perform repetitive tasks—studies have found that rewards don't undermine internal motivation to perform uninteresting tasks—but when applied to job functions that require innovation, these rewards can actually harm intrinsic motivation. If businesses want to move beyond the current landscape of employee malaise, identifying and catering to intrinsic motivation represents the only way forward. (Watson, 2014)

We would say the same applies to education. If students continuously ask, "What do I get?" they have been bribed or rewarded too often. Using rewards teaches students that what they *get* is more important than what they *do*.

Encouraging Unrealistic Expectations

Over time, students demand more stuff to perform the same activities. Many advocates of constant rewards and bribes believe it is easy to start with a prize of some kind when your student learns a skill; once the behavior or skill is learned, the student can be weaned from the reward. In fact, this rarely happens. Switching from external rewards to "doing it because it is the right thing to do" ignores how hard it is to break habits.

When one of us taught 7th grade, students received stickers as rewards for basic tasks. One day we unexpectedly ran out of stickers, and when the class was informed, a near-riot ensued. "Where's my sticker?" "I want a sticker!" "I won't do anything without a sticker!" A parent even called that night to complain that her child was upset because he hadn't been given his sticker! The main reason for using stickers is that they are a billion-dollar industry in the United States. Think of what that money might buy—more teacher aides; new books or equipment; and for some schools, air conditioning. We prefer things like these to stickers.

Sometimes a teacher may want to give a child or class a small gift to show appreciation, not to reward behavior. In some cases, this is a thoughtful and encouraging gesture by the teacher. But there are two hidden dangers to consider. If students come to expect that they will receive a gift for good behavior—and this can happen after only one gift—then the gift becomes an unintended manipulation. The student may think, "I got a gift the last time I did this. If I do it again, maybe I'll get another one." Although we believe that "fair" is not necessarily the same as "equal," we still think that not being equal is not always fair. Students who never get gifts may become less motivated. Is giving a gift as a form of appreciation worth it? It can be if it is genuine, unexpected, and a symbolic "thank-you" rather than the main currency of behavior management.

Creating Dependency

Having fewer decision-making opportunities for students leads to their dependency on adults. This problem is more serious when students become paralyzed about important decisions, including who to trust, what job to accept, and what college to attend. They become unable to make choices without another's approval.

Teachers do not create most cases of dependency, and although we don't want students to become overly dependent on teachers, we do need to acknowledge that teacher influence is still extremely important for student decision making. Students need to practice making independent decisions in our presence so they learn to make good decisions in our absence. If students need incentives to achieve or behave, they should identify a goal and reward themselves when they achieve it. Dependent students do not always rely on people who have their best interests in mind. When students are dependent, they look for stronger, charismatic, or popular people for direction. It is safer and healthier to reduce rewards so students learn to think for themselves at an early age. Dependency on rewards can result in addiction to rewards. The more students depend on rewards, the less they will do without them.

Rewards as Upside-Down Punishments

If you tell a student you'll give him a piece of candy if he answers all the questions on his paper and he doesn't do it, you then must tell him he can't get the candy. Is he more likely to think "I didn't earn a reward" or "I'm being punished"? Because we have the ability to give, we also have the ability to withhold. Reward and punishment are two sides of the same coin: the teacher is in control. The teacher might feel that the student chose to act in a way that led to withholding the reward. This is a logical assumption, because the teacher made clear the contingency for the candy and the student didn't earn it. However, feelings aren't always logical, especially among students. A few students might accept that they are responsible for not earning the reward; most others feel punished. Others might feel that their teachers are depriving them of something that they want and should have.

Manipulation

We do not like it when students try to manipulate us, yet we frequently employ manipulating strategies as teaching strategies. In doing so we teach students by example to be master manipulators. If your spouse or love interest gave you a desired present—a beautiful bouquet of flowers, for example—and then said "I love you" but an hour later asked you to do a big favor, would you feel loved or manipulated? Rewards that come with a "price tag" are a form of manipulation.

Students feel the same way when we give them something of value or do something nice for them and then use it against them when they refuse to do what we want. If you find yourself saying something like "I just put a gold star on your paper; why can't you clean your area?" you have engaged in pure manipulation, ruining your student's joy in knowing you cared enough to give a gold star. Sentences that start with "If you do ___, then you'll get ___" should be seen as a warning that you are about to manipulate your student. Avoid asking your students to do something soon after you give them something, be it a treat, a privilege, or a favored activity.

Teachers use praise and rewards in many different ways. If you ever pointed out how well one of your students is behaving in front of your other students to get the others to do the same ("Look how nicely Carrie is sitting at her table"), then don't be surprised when they do the same to you: "But Mrs. Robbins is letting her class leave five minutes early. Why can't we?"

Reducing Choices

When we offer an incentive for a student to do something, we obviously are deciding for that student what we want him to do. This is not inherently negative; often we need to make decisions for students, especially those affecting young students and those involving safety. Yet when we make decisions for others, we take away their ability to make their own choices, and we lose an opportunity to teach decision-making skills. One way to identify great teachers is by how well they balance telling students what to do and letting them make their own choices. Few teachers, if any, get the balance right all of the time. One of the best ways to achieve a healthy balance is to offer choices within limits the majority of times when control is a relevant issue.

Reducing choice is related to control-oriented teaching. It is not coincidental that the use of bribes and rewards goes hand in hand with the need to be in control. Eliminating or severely limiting choices for students lessens their world experience. Eliminating their sense of power and control through bribery eventually becomes unhealthy.

Rewards as Bribes to Do Something Undesirable

We've rarely heard a teacher say, "If you text your friends, I'll give you a treat." We generally do not reward students for doing what they love because we don't need to. They do what they love because they want to. We do, however, sometimes reward them for doing things that they do *not* want to do. We use bribes to get students to do what *we* want, knowing that they would refuse if given a choice. Students learn very quickly that a reward means "I'm being asked to do something I don't want to do." The message "something bad is coming your way" is frequently received even before students know what they will be asked to do.

A False Analogy

An argument that compares students and rewards with workers and salaries is one of the most common rationales for using rewards with students. It appears to make sense, yet it doesn't. A reward in school is used to shape a student's behavior and choices. A worker gets a salary for services provided. But here's the catch: workers choose their professions and therefore accept what will be required; no one makes them take any specific job or work at a specific place. Although the economy might restrict many possible choices, workers still do not have to take a job if they choose not to. Students, on the other hand, cannot choose a different teacher if they don't want to behave the way a particular teacher wants them to.

Rewards and Low Expectations

When teachers set the bar for earning a reward, students rarely go beyond what's needed to obtain that reward. But when students are internally motivated, there is no telling how much they might achieve both academically and behaviorally. For example, one of the authors wrote 10 extra questions on a final examination. Students earned no extra points for answering them; there was absolutely no benefit except seeing if they understood the concept raised by the question. All but a few students answered some of the questions, and many answered all of them. Without a limit imposed by a reward, students chose to go much farther.

Appreciation, Not Reward

The following guidelines can help you to decide how to appreciate and encourage students with minimal manipulation:

1. Recognize that true appreciation is a feeling, not a strategy. Children need to know that their efforts are appreciated. We cannot survive psychologically without knowing that we are appreciated.

Unlike rewards, encouragement is not meant to manipulate. It is meant to show positive regard, not to obtain a specified result.

2. Make your statement to your student *after* the behavior you wish to comment on, not before. It is better to say "I'm proud of what you did" than "I expect you to do a good job."

3. Don't make your appreciation conditional. Anything you say that has a condition attached is a reward, not a shared feeling. Conditionals can easily be recognized by their "if-then" construction: "If you sit without tapping, then I'll be proud of you," or "If you don't interrupt, then you can play a game before our class ends."

4. Start by expressing how you feel. After all, the point of an appreciation is to share genuine feelings. Say something like "I feel (noticed that, saw you) ___" instead of "You should (ought to, must) ___."

5. Be random and unexpected with your comments. You can keep your students from becoming dependent on validation if they don't always expect it.

6. Recognize that giving with no request for something in return is called appreciation. We are all in favor of this. Tell students with passion, energy, and emotion how proud of them you are. Tell them when you feel sad, disappointed, or angry. Feelings last. Explain what expressing positive feelings means. Students and staff need to feel appreciated and encouraged.

7. Be genuine. Don't offer an appreciation as a strategy to guide your students, but as an opportunity to engage in honest communication.

8. Expect nothing in return. Avoid saying things like "I gave you time to talk with your friends yesterday. Why can't you pay attention now?"

9. Understand that it's OK to give unexpected small gifts to a student, as long as the gift isn't payment for a desired behavioral outcome. Your students deserve knowing that their accomplishments matter to you.

10. Acknowledge that it's OK to celebrate an achievement. Events that are cause for celebration include graduating from 6th grade or high school, winning an important game, or solving a difficult computer problem. Don't deny your students the joy of celebration because you fear rewarding them.

11. Don't use sweets, salty snacks, or pizza as rewards. Instead, use healthful foods like fruit and veggies. When children learn that unhealthy foods are an option, they will reward themselves with those foods outside school.

By and large, the message you want to send when using rewards is this: "I expect you to behave and follow rules because that is the right thing to do. Understand that even though I may not always tell you, I always appreciate when my students do the right thing. Occasionally I may want to thank you with a free homework pass or in some other way, but don't expect it. In fact, if you ask for those things, the answer will be no."

Even when we learn better ways to discipline, it takes courage to change.

Final Thoughts

On an episode of his podcast *Revisionist History,* Malcolm Gladwell (2016) talks with economist and behavioral scientist Richard H. Thayer about why people do things in ways that they know are inferior to other methods. The upshot is, most value approval from bosses or peers more than achieving a successful outcome. Applying Thayer and Gladwell's theory to teachers, we see that when teachers have a choice between peer acceptance and administrative support versus success in the classroom, many choose the former. For these teachers, the pain of being ostracized by peers is stronger than the pleasure they derive from their students' success. To overcome this tendency, we urge seeking administrative support by explaining what you are doing and why you are doing it differently. Nobody knows your class better than you do, but you are unlikely to receive support unless you explain how the new method is facilitating greater student success or better behavior—or both. As for peer support, you are likely to find that if your method achieves sustained success, at least some colleagues will want to connect with you.

4

The Keys to Changing Behavior

At our seminars we ask participants to raise their hands if they have tried to change something either big or little about themselves during the last year or two. Because we are simply interested in having them realize how widespread the desire for change is within the group, we do not ask them to tell us what kind of change they seek. Virtually everyone raises a hand. We then ask if the change process went smoothly and easily. At most, one or two raise their hands, and we congratulate them on their quick success. The vast majority acknowledge difficulties either making the change or, more commonly, sticking with the change. As an example, most people agree that just about anybody can stick with any diet for one hour. More difficult is sticking with it for a full day, and much more difficult is doing so for a week, a month, or a year. The point of the exercise is to acknowledge that even when people are motivated to change, making change happen and sustaining it are very difficult and sometimes impossible. If it is that hard for adults to change when they want to, how hard must it be to get *children* to change when they *don't* want to?

When deciding what to do with a child whose behavior is unacceptable, it is essential to first understand that changing behaviors is a roller-coaster ride. The roller-coaster analogy also applies while brainstorming proper strategies to stimulate this change. If a student has a calm Monday, do not be surprised if he is disruptive on Tuesday. For some students, it is literally one good hour followed by one bad hour. Be prepared for this effect. As with the stock market, the goal is to move in a positive direction—which usually does happen over the long haul, but not without encountering dips and occasional plunges. In the following sections, we present some essential truths and understandings to keep in mind.

Realize That Nobody Can Really Change Somebody Else

We've already noted a critical question that expresses the difficulty of changing behavior: If we can't always change our own behavior when we want to, how can we change another's behavior when that person might not want to change? The fact is, we can't. This reality can guide our interactions with disruptive youngsters. When students say, "You can't make me!" avoid responding with a demand or threat. Doing so is likely to lead to a power struggle. Instead, acknowledge that they are correct. With passion and sincerity say, "You're right. Only you can make yourself change, and I hope you will. I believe in you. I will be here if you need help." This response recognizes and respects the child's need for power and control and seeks to explain rather than threaten. The goal is to show the student how it is in his best interest to make a different choice.

Figure Out What Is at the Core of the Unacceptable Behavior

It is unreasonable to expect any technique, strategy, method, or philosophy to work with all people who present the same problem. Chest pain might be a symptom of simple indigestion, acid reflux, a heart attack, a tumor, or a strained muscle. Like a competent physician who needs to get at the source to best treat the symptom, educators should understand the reasons or functions of a behavior to formulate a strategy that is likely to work.

In general, the driving forces of inappropriate behaviors are the unfulfilled needs for *attention, connection, identity, competence, control,* and *fun.* Two students might show the same outward behavior, such as refusing to work, but one might believe himself to be incapable (an issue of competence), while the other is defiant (an issue of control). These students need different solutions even though they show the same outward behavior. Fear, frustration, and anger are among the emotions triggered when basic needs are not met. In Chapter 6 (formal discipline methods), we explain why you can't always treat everyone the same way.

Recognize the Difference Between Two Basic Change Strategies: *Leverage* and *Persuasion*

When one of us was consulting at a middle school in a neighborhood filled with gangs, drugs, and poverty, a walk on the campus with the assistant principal led to a challenging situation. We came upon a teacher and a student in a heated argument:

Teacher: You can't talk to me that way.

Jose: Yes, I can. You're a damn liar.

Teacher: I said you can't talk to me that way!

Jose: You're a damn liar.

Teacher: If you say that again, I'll make sure you don't go on to 8th grade.

Jose: You're a damn liar.

As I entered this argument, I asked the teacher if I could talk with Jose privately. "Somebody better talk to him!" she growled. I was thrilled. For two years, I'd been giving teachers suggestions on how to deal with students like Jose. Now I had my chance to validate everything I had been saying. I was sure that the story of my positive influence would spread around the school in a matter of hours.

Jose and I walked into an empty room. This is the gist of our conversation:

Me: Why are you so angry at that teacher?

Jose: Because she insulted me.

Me: Is it wrong to insult people?

Jose: Yes.

Me: Is it always wrong?

Jose: Yes.

Me: But calling your teacher a liar is an insult, isn't it? Isn't that an insult?

Jose: That's different.

After a long conversation, we agreed that the best way for him to win was to apologize for calling his teacher a liar, but he would still say she was wrong. We practiced for a while, and he proudly announced, "I'm ready. I can do this." We approached his teacher, and the following exchange took place:

Me: Jose has something to tell you.

Jose: You're a damn fuckin' liar.

Me: (In shock) That's not what we practiced.

Jose: Who the fuck are you? She's a fuckin' liar, and I'm not changing my mind!

Needless to say, this incident was more than a bit embarrassing. It also proves that no matter how good we are and how much work we do, students cannot be forced or always influenced to change.

Having *leverage* means having and using power to get what we want from someone else. It relies heavily on threats, punishments, and bribes because it is dependent on pain or pleasure for success. At school, it can only be an effective method of change if the child wants what is offered (e.g., stickers) more than whatever gratification is achieved by the behavior, or wants to avoid something sufficiently unpleasant to interrupt whatever fulfillment the undesired behavior provides. For example, "time out" is only effective with students who prefer "time in." A child has to like recess in order for its removal to have an impact. Leverage is usually easier and takes less time than other methods because it doesn't rely much, if at all, on good teacher-student relationships. Unfortunately, it is also far less effective with students who are regularly difficult because they don't care about most traditional punishments.

Persuasion is helping students see how the proposed change is in their best interest. It relies heavily on listening to what the child is seeking through the inappropriate behavior. Its strategies include logic, emotion, and connection. Persuasion can be about explaining and providing examples of how the change will benefit a person's life in a way that makes sense. For example, in dealing with a high school student who has no motivation to make an effort in class, you might say something like this: "Not only will you make a lot more money as a high school graduate than as a dropout, but if you change your behavior, you're less likely to get nagged and picked at, which you hate."

Persuasion can also be about enhancing someone's awareness of how the consequences of the current disruptive behavior lead to unwanted feelings (emotions). For example, "Expressing anger by slamming books and yelling creates problems for you even if the teacher is being unfair. Would you like to look at some other ways to express your feelings that most teachers would find more respectful?"

We have a better chance of influencing behavior when students trust us, want our approval, or want to avoid disappointing us. For example, expressing disappointment to a child for using unacceptable language is likely to register if the child feels connected to the teacher, believes the teacher cares about him, and knows a more acceptable way to say the same thing.

Persuasion strategies help students *want to change*, not because of fear, loss of reward, or punishment, but because they choose to behave differently. Their success relies heavily on instilling hope or the belief that life can get better. This change in internal motivation is not easy, but it is possible.

Students are more likely to be persuaded when they understand why a change makes sense. Simply telling a student to do something without discussing why it is worth doing has only a short-term benefit at best. Showing how the behavioral change will directly help the student rather than only make life better for you or others increases the chances for success. For example, a student is much more likely to complete an assignment when she realizes that success is probable with reasonable effort.

Sometimes it is best to ask students why *they* think adapting to changes we want to make will be beneficial to them. We've witnessed a helpful classroom game called "Tell Us Why It's Better." Prepare a list of certain behaviors covered by procedures and rules. Then ask students individually or collectively why they think it is better to do those things than to not do them. Here are some examples:

Why is it *better* . . .
- To do your homework?
- To help another student?
- To help clean up your things?
- To admit when you're wrong?
- To share with your friends?
- To be on time for class?
- To tell the truth about what you do?
- To use your words when you are angry?

Change can be approached from the inside out and from the outside in. *Inside-out* change methods view the student as the problem and therefore require the student to change from within to adapt to the demands of school. Actions are done *to* or *with* the student with the expectation that the student will change the undesirable behavior. Nothing is changed within the system. Interventions might include counseling, reminders, warnings, rewards, time-outs, behavior plans, detentions, and suspensions. All are designed to alter the student's behavior without expecting any fundamental system change. *Outside-in* change looks at factors within the school, such as the behavior of the teacher, other students, parents, and the curriculum to influence change. Consider the following example.

Deshaun rarely participates in class and is often out of his seat disturbing others. When the teacher corrects him, he claims that she always picks on him. Things quickly escalate and often lead to his being removed from class. The counselor works with Deshaun and teaches him that he is less likely to get into trouble if he uses a method called "SLANT" (Meier, 2013) when the teacher is teaching. SLANT is an acronym for **S**it up straight/**S**mile; **L**isten; **A**sk one specific question; **N**od to show interest; **T**rack the teacher. The counselor teaches and practices with him, and he starts using the method. He gets a positive response from his teacher and gets into less trouble. This is an *inside-out* strategy because Deshaun has learned and is using a strategy to change himself. In contrast, *outside-in* strategies require change within the system that might influence behavior, such as the teacher enhancing her relationship with him, correcting him privately instead of publicly, or modifying the curriculum to fit his strengths. To facilitate the most effective and long-lasting changes, it is often best to explore inside-out and outside-in methods simultaneously.

Understand That Many People Resist Change When They Feel Forced to Let Go of the Familiar

Don't expect most students to let go of an old behavior until they learn, practice, and integrate something new. These efforts take time, and while the student is learning a new behavior, prepare for the roller-coaster experience discussed earlier. Invite students to try a new behavior rather than demand they do so. Here's an example of how that might be expressed: "Showing that you are tough is important so people don't mess with you. You have what it takes. Fighting at school makes problems for you. You get sent to the office. You get suspended. You miss class. You get farther behind. You end up failing. The only person you hurt is you. Want to learn how to stand up for yourself in a way that makes you look tough and doesn't break the rules?"

Show Students They Already Have What It Takes

In an interview concerning his recovery from substance abuse, actor Richard Dreyfuss said, "There's nothing wrong with scrutinizing yourself as closely as you can. When you do that, especially with help from an intelligent doctor, you can find little parts of your day that you accomplished something, and you can build on that. That's something that makes a difference" (PBS, 2016). Dreyfuss's observation makes the point that it is much easier to build on a skill that is already present than it is to give birth to something new. Like an "intelligent doctor," teachers facilitate change when they closely scrutinize a child's behavior looking for growth and then make the child aware that she already has what it takes. When you see a student acting in a way that deserves encouragement, let her know and make her aware. For example, "Marty, I noticed this morning during class that you ignored Ann when she annoyed you. You seemed able to get on with your work without anybody reminding you. I know you've been working on that. What did you do to make it happen?" Notice that along with expressing appreciation and encouragement for showing improvement, asking "What did you do?" turns attention inward. Lasting change happens when students attribute change to their own effort.

Don't Require a Forever Goodbye

When it comes to change, there are leapers and toe-dippers. Leapers make wholesale changes right away. Toe-dippers acclimate little by little. For example, leapers who want to stop smoking often throw away all cigarettes, thinking they will never smoke again. Unfortunately, this approach rarely lasts more than a few days for most people because the thought of *never* smoking again can feel like losing a friend. Changing from "never again" to "one day at a time" makes the task feel less overwhelming.

The "one day at a time" mantra of many habit-breaking recovery programs provides a good model for use with students who are "addicted" to inappropriate behavior. For example, Ms. Smith enthusiastically challenges her student Alex by saying, "We both know silent reading is tough for you, so I want to challenge you to stay seated and really work for 10 minutes before getting up." After 10 minutes, she says, "Alex, that was cool. You did it. By the way, if you absolutely have to get up and stretch, go ahead and stretch; but it would be great to see another 5 minutes. That would be a new record for you! Can you go for it?"

When using a gradual process for breaking the cycle of bad behavior, sometimes it is better to break a task down into smaller, more manageable steps and build over time to the final goal. For example, instead of telling a student to do his entire homework assignment, say, "Tonight just do one problem. When you're finished, check your answer against mine."

Define a Beginning and an End

Have you ever waited for a delayed flight or a doctor running late? Although waiting is not fun, not knowing the departure time or when the doctor will call can be worse than the actual wait. Most people would rather wait two hours knowing the exact time a flight leaves than spend an hour waiting without knowing how long the wait will be. Csikszentmihalyi (1990) applied this phenomenon to tasks in general, and we can apply this knowledge to the behaviors we want to change in our students. We are most likely to succeed if we ask for a behavior change within a defined time or quantity. For example, we can allow a student who incessantly asks questions to ask a limited number of questions within a defined time frame. With guidance, many students, depending on age and ability, can participate in setting their own limits.

Use Challenge to Promote Change

A great way to change behavior is through challenge. Every person responds to challenge in one form or another. The level of the challenge and its connection to the person should be a good fit. As an analogy, look at how students select electronic games. If the game is too easy, they feel no pride in winning and plenty of humiliation in losing; in addition, it quickly becomes boring to play. If the game is too hard, many give up. The best games are hard enough so there is pride in winning, but not so hard that winning is impossible. Students are very good at finding their own best challenge in multiple-level games because they'll keep playing at the same level until they've mastered it before moving to the next.

The same concept and strategy can be used to help motivate a student to change. We can turn new behaviors into challenges that inspire pride. Here are some examples of using challenge to change behavior:

"It takes a lot of courage not to hit when you're angry; I wonder how brave you can be."

"There is nothing harder than not smoking when your friends do. Do you think you can say no?"

"I'm curious to see if you can do two more problems tonight than you did yesterday."

"I can think of three ways to solve this problem. They are (1) ___, (2) ___, and (3) ___. How many more can you add?"

"You read two books last summer. I wonder if you can read three this summer."

(After a student shouts something mean at you) "It takes a lot of courage to tell me how you really feel, and I respect that. It takes even more courage to wait until we are alone so you can hear my side of the story, too."

"Few students your age can do what I'm about to ask, but I think you're old enough to try. Are you interested in doing what older students can do?"

Practice speaking these examples aloud, because voice tone, body language, and proximity matter. The idea is to provide new ways for students to face behavior issues. Two of the best challenges for younger students are connected to age and courage. Students like proving they can do what older students do and that they are brave. By challenging instead of demanding, the change becomes more internally pleasing when accomplished because the student has proven to himself he can do it. A feeling of pride accompanies success.

We strongly advise against telling students that something is easy. For example, "Guys, I know you are not happy about taking this test, but I promise it is really not that hard." If we say the task is easy, students feel little pride in accomplishing it. They have nothing to gain. If they try and don't succeed, failure leads to shame, frustration, and humiliation. Labeling a task "easy" offers little to gain and much to lose. This is one reason some students refuse to do easy things. Instead, say, "If you try, you can feel proud. Do not worry about success or failure. Effort is what matters. Failing is part of success, but quitting is not!" With that kind of support, students have a lot to gain and very little to lose.

Ask, Is the Desired Change Happening?

Most of the time it is neither practical nor possible to do a controlled study at school to assess the effectiveness of a program or technique in every classroom, with every child. That said, it is important to know if we are achieving the desired result. Too often, either because we don't know what else to do or out of habit, we do things that don't work. We recommend trying a strategy at least five times or staying committed for a minimum of three weeks. It should be clear by the fifth zero in the grade book that a zero is not an effective strategy to get a student to do homework. Look for the roller coaster. If you're seeing ups and downs, stay on the path. If you're seeing no improvement, consider tweaking without abandoning. Check with a resource professional at the school to ensure your goals are reasonable.

Expect to Feel Uncomfortable

We usually feel comfortable in familiar situations. When comfort leads to success or happiness, the result is satisfying. When comfort does not get us the desired result—such as improving the behavior of challenging students—we get frustrated. Frustration can lead to a fractured relationship if neither student nor teacher is willing to do something different. Somebody has to change for things to improve.

Because it is easiest to change ourselves, we recommend starting there. Discomfort can lead to constructively trying new things with the possibility of a better outcome. Keep in mind that mastering new behaviors takes lots of practice and patience. When working at a juvenile detention facility with teen boys who often arrived without appropriate social skills, one of us was initially aghast when they told him to "fuck off" or "flipped him the bird." Only after practicing "desensitization" by using a mirror to "flip himself off" numerous times was he able to unemotionally get outside himself and focus on the child's issues. If what you're doing isn't working, consider a change in attitude, strategy, or both to push beyond your comfort zone and possibly gain a better outcome.

Realize That Students Must Learn and Practice Something to Get Better at It

Like us, students are likely to feel uncomfortable when asked to change. Like us, they need opportunities to practice a new behavior. We often tell students what to do without demonstrating and then require them to practice the specifics. One rule for behavior change is this: every time we take something away from a student, we must replace it with something else. Students who run in the halls should be taught and expected to practice walking. A student who loses her temper needs to be taught ways to calm herself and use appropriate language to express frustration. Too often, schools punish students by removing privileges or placing them in a contained setting without teaching more acceptable alternatives and providing opportunities for practice. Before telling students to stop fighting, have some acceptable alternatives in mind and share those.

Practicing the things we fail at is one of the most important components of success. Imagine saying to a basketball player, "Because you missed so many shots during the game, you are forbidden to shoot until you improve," or to a pianist, "Because you are so bad at playing the piano, until you get better, you can't play." These statements are ridiculous. The response would be "How can I get better if I don't practice?" The only way to get better at something is to do more of it. These examples show that without opportunities to learn and practice, it is impossible to improve. Yet in school we say things like "These students don't know how to play appropriately during recess, so until they do, there'll be no recess." It is not possible to get better at anything without learning a better way and then doing more of it. The principle that no one can improve without repetition puts into question a common classroom technique of denying the opportunity to learn a better way. Do any of the following examples sound familiar?

"You can't go on the field trip because I don't trust you."

"This is your third 'late.' Don't bother coming until you can be on time."

"You can't go to the assembly because you always interrupt it."

The best way for students to learn how to behave in these environments is through role-play (practicing acceptable behavior in class) and role-reversal (assuming the role of the student doing what you disapprove of while letting the student practice teaching you what you want him to do) until sufficient mastery of the new behavior is evident.

Do What You Tell Your Students to Do

The principal of an alternative school told us he called in the mother of a student who had been fighting. The mother casually strolled over to her child and slapped him hard across the face as she scolded, "Who taught you to hit?"

As most teachers realize but don't always demonstrate, modeling how we want students to behave may be the most powerful tool we have. Like it or not, students are constantly watching how we behave in difficult situations. They absorb, mimic, and respond to what they see. Some students behave like their teachers, while others consciously rebel. None of us can be perfect in front of our students, but students can't be perfect in front of us, either. In general, if we yell, so will they; if we interrupt them, they will often do the same to us. If we are lazy about grading papers and returning student work, we should not be surprised if students are not prompt. We help create sarcastic students by being sarcastic with them. If we want students to say "please," "thank you," and "good morning," we should be sure to use these words and greet them this way every day. If we don't want students to be late for class, we should be ready with an engaging activity as soon as the class begins. We should avoid being late handing back tests and papers. If we make a promise, we should keep it.

Obviously adults get more privileges than students: the right to drive, to vote, to drink alcoholic beverages, to marry, and to stay up late, among others. But it is important to keep adult privileges from becoming one set of rules for us and another for students. If they aren't allowed to eat, drink, or chew gum in class, we shouldn't do these things, either. If we strive to have them be kind to one another and avoid using put-downs, we must hold ourselves to the same standard. If we break one of our own rules, we should explain why we considered it necessary or apologize without making excuses or blaming others.

What does all this mean for teachers? Visible actions related to values are much louder and more compelling than words. If you value reading, let students watch you read. Tell the truth, even when it is inconvenient, especially in seemingly small situations. Don't contradict values with actions. We once saw a car with a bumper sticker that said "Say no to drugs" as cigarette smoke poured out the window.

Modeling can be used as a filter. Ask yourself when you interact with your students, "Do I want my students to do what I'm about to do?" "Do I want my student to say what I'm about to say and in the way I'm about to say it?" "Do I tell students one thing and do something contrary?" Think of the way you treat students when they misbehave. Do you want them to mimic you when they feel others have misbehaved toward them? If you yell, "Stop that right now!" do you want them to yell the same to a friend?

Self-reflection is a helpful skill to teach. If students see us pause and reflect in real-life situations, they will have an opportunity to incorporate such behavior into the way they interact with others. Teach them to write angry letters that they never send instead of lashing out or hitting when angry. Have practice dialogues when a teacher or friend upsets them so they can let off steam in the presence of someone who really listens. Give them a stuffed animal to hug really tightly or a towel to squeeze when upset.

Students want to be adults. They learn how by watching and copying the adults who have the greatest influence on them. With the power of our actions as examples, students can learn to navigate the incredible number of choices before them. The world may be evolving in ways that are so fast and confusing that it can be hard to find the best way forward. Thankfully, modeling is a stable pathway, unaffected by technology, economics, or politics. It always works—no matter what the world becomes.

5

The Power of Prevention

It is rare for any teacher to go through an entire school year and have all students show up on time, do their work, get along with one another, keep impulses in check, and disagree respectfully when having different points of view. This book includes many strategies that can help educators effectively handle disruptions and behavior problems that seem almost inevitable. However, we prefer creating an environment that focuses on *prevention*—taking steps to prevent behavior problems from occurring rather than resolving them after they occur.

Basic Needs That Drive Behavior

Prevention begins by realizing that some students will come to school with unfulfilled basic needs and severe social-skill deficits that motivate them to act inappropriately. The unfulfilled needs that are the underlying cause of misbehavior are the following:

- Identity
- Attention
- Connection
- Competence
- Control
- Fun

Prevention prepares educators to implement strategies and interventions to address these needs, thus getting at the root of the problem. The best way to resolve and prevent a needs-based problem is to find ways to meet the need instead of challenging it. Your goal is always to keep problems from occurring or escalating.

Identity

Identity refers to how we view ourselves and how we feel about ourselves. We all have an image of ourselves. In school-age children, these images change rapidly and are very fragile. When teachers take time to notice how students feel about themselves and connect with those feelings, many behavior problems can be avoided. For example, if you know that a student is having a "bad hair day," tell her you have far too many bad hair days yourself and ask for advice on how to deal with it. When students learn to accept who they are and understand that they can use that reality for their benefit or they can change some things about the way they act, they take control of their own needs. Remind them that, for example, pimples don't last forever; being laughed at can change to being funny; no one is the only student in class with a weight problem. One way to help students form a healthy self-concept is by changing the way they think of themselves when challenged. For example, you can help a student who lacks friends to develop some friendships, but at the same time ask her to think of three things she enjoys about being alone.

Attention

Attention is the need to be acknowledged by others in a way that makes us feel that we matter. The psychiatrist and writer Rollo May (1969) once wrote that being bad is always better than being ignored. Call more often on students who need attention, ask them to comment on other students' answers in discussions, greet them at the door, and smile at them when you're cruising around the classroom.

Connection

Connection refers to our need to feel that we belong to something that matters to us. In some cases, the group that a troubled student is most connected to consists of other troubled students. For example, Eric Harris and Dylan Klebold, the perpetrators of the Columbine shooting massacre in 1999, were thought to be part of a group they called the Trench Coat Mafia. Their connection led to a horror. Often, students choose friends with similar problems rather than similar interests. You can minimize destructive connections by resolving conflicts in ways that don't alienate your students. You can also try to connect troubled youth to more positive groups like sport teams, school theater programs, or music ensembles. You can also make personal connections with students who need an adult connection. Without becoming friends, you can show interest, take a student under your wing, or check in often to see how the student is doing.

Competence

Competence is about feeling that we know how do to something and have the skills necessary for success. When achievement is considered the most important measure of success, many students will not develop a sense of competence. That's why throughout this book we continually stress effort as the primary measure of success.

Control

Control is based on the desire to make decisions that count, to have real choices, and to control our environment. Like the rest of us, students fight the feeling of helplessness. Symptoms of not feeling enough control are expressed when students say things like "You're not the boss of me" or "You can't make me." Students lacking a sense of control are frequently bossy with others and tend to get into power struggles with authority. Power often means having the power to choose within limits among alternatives. The more choices you give to students with power issues, the fewer problems they will create. Give them choices both academically and behaviorally. Be careful your choices aren't disguised threats (see pp. 26–28). Instead of demanding that a student sit down, offer a choice: "You can sit down now, or take a few minutes standing in the back of the room where you won't interrupt the lesson. Which makes the most sense to you?"

Fun

Fun is a need we all have. The more fun school is, the fewer difficult issues teachers face. Many teachers say that not all learning is fun; sometimes you just have to do the work even when it is not pleasurable. We don't disagree. Hard work can't always be fun. However, if teachers focus as much on *how* to teach as they do on *what* to teach, all lessons can include an element of fun. Take math, for example. You can teach basic arithmetic or complex algebra by showing equations on the board ($3 + 4 = 7$), or you can ask some students to stand and ask other students to move them around to demonstrate the equation. Both methods teach the same mathematical function, but only one includes an element of fun.

The prevention mind-set is largely responsible for the early and sustained success of Discipline with Dignity. Looking at prevention from the student perspective, appropriate behavior is generally achieved when students

• Feel connected to the teacher, one another, and the curriculum.
• Believe that success is attainable with reasonable effort.
• Feel respected by being heard; feel teachers strongly care about them in personal ways.
• Are given responsibility, especially in helping other children.
• Look forward to sanctioned moments of joy and laughter every day.
• Believe that what is taught is relevant to something they care about.

Six Things Teachers Can Do to Prevent Discipline Problems

Figure 5.1 is a personal survey that incorporates practices associated with discipline prevention. We suggest you use it to assess what you currently do well and what you should consider giving more of your attention. The survey statements can be synthesized into six basic things that teachers can do to minimize discipline problems in the classroom. Let's look at each of these in turn.

Figure 5.1
Self-Survey on Prevention Practices

Ask yourself: Which of the following practices do you do well? Which can you improve to prevent discipline problems?

__ I usually correct behavior in a dignified way.

__ I encourage students to work independently in self-directed activities.

__ I find ways to like students who try to make themselves unlikable.

__ I allow my students to make some decisions about classroom management.

__ I allow my students to openly disagree with me.

__ I greet students regularly.

__ I laugh a lot in class.

__ I regularly connect with my difficult students around something that interests them.

__ I allow students to redo, retake, and revise their work to improve grades.

__ When I have a problem with a student, I take some responsibility for contributing to it.

__ I call parents at least twice to share something positive before I seek help with a problem.

__ I have a suggestion box in my class and ask students to contribute ideas they think will make the class an even better place.

__ I tell my students what they do that I like, and ask what they like about others and about me.

__ I give my students some say in the content that I teach.

__ My students are involved in developing values, rules, and consequences.

Pick one survey statement that identifies something you want to do more of, and list three specific steps to get it done:

1.

2.

3.

Make Connecting with Students a Top Priority

The more aware you are of your students, their surroundings, their culture, and their home lives, the more *connected* they feel. We recently observed in intermediate-level classrooms of teachers who had asked for assistance with one or more of their difficult students. We saw a range of inappropriate behaviors, including Keegan wandering around the room, Carlton with his head on the desk, Shaleesha and Louisa bickering over a pencil, and Manny making squeaky noises. Later we met with each teacher to discuss concerns and explore strategies. Although each teacher had no trouble reciting a litany of disruptions these students caused, not one was able to tell us a favorite out-of-school interest, hobby, or activity enjoyed by any of them. Ask students questions. If they do not respond, answer your own question. Doing so will usually move them to add to or correct what you've said, which can provide you with useful information.

We realize it is unfair to generalize from this small sample, but these five teachers, although frustrated, seemed like caring people dedicated to helping their students. When asked, each teacher believed he or she had a good relationship with the most disruptive student in each class. We decided to ask each student the same question. Surprisingly, four out of five believed their teacher did not truly care about them. In fact, in a national survey of students in grades 6 through 12 conducted by the Pearson Foundation (2014), fewer than half believed their teachers cared about them and would feel comfortable approaching their teachers with a problem. We believe the numbers are significantly lower among the behaviorally challenging population. Yet when we do informal surveys of teachers, almost all claim to care about all of their students. Why is there this disconnect, and what can we do about it? How well do *you* know your challenging students? To find out, we recommend completing the Student Knowledge Inventory (Figure 5.2).

The "2-question quiz" is a quick way to learn how your students perceive you as a teacher. Offer each student a blank note card. On Side A are spaces for students to respond to the question "What are two things about me as a teacher you love?" On Side B are spaces for students to respond to the question "What are two things about me as

Figure 5.2
Student Knowledge Inventory

Write the name of one of your favorite students on the top of Column 1 and the name of one of your least favorite students on the top of Column 2. Answer the related questions about each student as best you can.

Favorite Student: **Least Favorite Student:**

_____   _____

Favorite in-school activity:

_____   _____

Favorite hobby:

_____   _____

Favorite television show:

_____   _____

Favorite music group or
video game:

_____   _____

Best friend (name):

_____   _____

One thing this student likes
about your class:

_____   _____

One thing this student
dislikes about your class:

_____   _____

One short-range goal:

_____   _____

One long-range goal:

_____   _____

Skill he or she is most
proud of:

_____   _____

Questions

1. Which student do I know more about?

2. Which student do I spend more positive time with?

3. What specific steps might I take to interact more positively with my difficult students?

    a. I will _____

    b. I will _____

    c. I will _____

4. What might I do less of with difficult students to get to better know their strengths?

    a. I will _____

    b. I will _____

    c. I will _____

For one week, keep a record of how often you do your six "I wills." See if anything changes.

Change That Was Expected:

Positive: _____

_____

Negative: _____

_____

Change That Was Unexpected:

Positive: _____

_____

Negative: _____

_____

a teacher you do not like?" Let them know you are serious about being a good teacher, so their answers matter.

We cannot stress strongly enough the importance of a caring connection. In fact, it is virtually impossible for vulnerable students to achieve school success without it unless they are fortunate to have a bright mind that learns quickly or mentoring from a trusted and credible individual who supports school achievement. Educators rarely directly face the reality that there are some students who succeed in making themselves hard to like. In life outside school, we are free to associate with people we like and to minimize or avoid contact with those we don't. Yet on "company time," we must strive to turn feelings of frustration, disappointment, and dread into feelings of excitement, hope, and challenge. Doing so requires taking good emotional care of ourselves (see Chapter 9 on stress) so that we don't simply give up.

Visualizing an "oppositional defiant" student as a "tenacious leader" demonstrating mental toughness might enable us to respond differently. For example, "Joey, I know I cannot force you to work because you have a strong mind of your own, but I can *ask* you to do a few problems. If you continue to do nothing, I won't know if I am being a good teacher for you. Consider yourself asked." Then walk away. Do not stand over the student waiting for him to comply.

When caring is the foundation of correcting, tough students usually respond more appropriately. The following questions can help you define how well you know a student: Do you know what the student is afraid of? Proud of? Anxious to talk about? Interests, dreams, and disappointments? Do you openly share who you are? If not, students may view you as someone trying to wield power and see you as yet another enemy to be resisted.

Many gang members and imprisoned teenagers value loyalty. Some would even choose death before ratting out a friend. When difficult students believe their teachers are loyal, they connect more quickly. Loyalty is built by telling the truth even when it's hard to do so, by respectfully disagreeing when they are wrong and refusing to give up on them when they quit on themselves. Most important, loyalty is built by standing with people when things are not going well.

A high school teacher recently told us that when she began to greet each of her challenging students every day with an *H*—"hello," "how are you?" handshake, high five—she was amazed at the positive changes that resulted. She had to consciously remind herself to say and do these things, as they were not part of her curriculum.

The lessons for teachers are simple: Be friendly. Smile. Nod when a student is talking to you. Listen closely to students' problems. Compliment them often. ("I notice you are wearing a new shirt. That color looks really good on you." "Are those new earrings? Where did you get them?") Express empathy if a student is having a rough time. Make yourself available to talk about anything other than school. Learn about hopes ("If you could spend more time with one person, who would it be?") and dreams ("When I was a kid, I remember wanting to be a musician. What about you?") Share your stories of success and failure. Naturally, good judgment is necessary when interacting in a more personal way. For example, try to avoid being alone in a room with a student. If a student needs extra help, go to a public place or one with surveillance. When sharing personal stories, younger teachers who work with teens should be friendly and welcoming but also clear about boundaries to avoid triggering adolescent fantasies.

Remember that developing strong personal relationships is like making small regular deposits in a bank account. They may seem insignificant at first, but over time they accumulate to produce wealth. When a withdrawal is needed, it's nice to know the funds are there.

Know and Express Yourself—Warts and All

Teachers who let down their defenses so students get to know them in their full humanity overwhelmingly have the fewest problems with discipline and motivation. They are comfortable in their own skin and able to own up when they blow it and know it. They are unafraid to acknowledge imperfections and realize that by acknowledging them, they actually connect much better with all students. For example, "I messed up yesterday, Dylan, and I owe you an apology. I lost my temper and called you out in front of your friends. That wasn't right. I need to work harder on staying in control. Now that you know how I feel, is there anything you can do differently that might keep us from getting this upset?" (See the "lowering shields" intervention on page 105.) Tough students benefit from seeing that we don't have to be perfect to be successful.

Let students know about your outside interests, passions, and preferences by bringing them to life in the moment. Mr. Jessup, a high school teacher who rarely has discipline problems, has pictures of his family and friends interspersed with photos of students scattered around his classroom. A big *Star Wars* fan, he has posters, character figures, and other memorabilia prominently displayed. At least three times during each class period he mixes a personal story into the lesson.

One way we express ourselves is through the clothes we wear. As teachers, our clothes should be appropriate. A principal we know has a rule for his staff: When you get dressed, raise your hands as high as possible. Then bend over to pick up a piece of paper. He says, "If I can see any part of butts or guts, it is inappropriate."

Difficult students in particular need to know that we have feelings, concerns, and uncertainties. They need to see and learn that we can get angry, express that anger, and still really care. They need to have expectations clearly communicated in a straightforward way. Use "I" statements to share how you are affected by the things they do: "I appreciate your saying that"; "I find those words hurtful." They need to hear your feelings (within limits), as in these examples:

"I love how much you want to share, but please raise your hand."

"I want you to talk and tell me how you feel and what you want rather than giving me dirty looks, slamming the door, and not doing your work. Will you talk with me after class?"

"I am very upset and so are you. I am walking away because that is what I tell you to do when you get angry. Wow! It is not as easy as I make it seem!"

"I am so angry right now at your disrespectful behavior that I feel like exploding, but I will try really hard not to, because I think you must be very unhappy to act this way. I hope after class you let me know what is going on. I hope you can act in a way we can both be proud of for the remainder of class."

Many of the students we are writing about in this book did not become the way they are overnight. We cannot expect them to change overnight. What we are asking of them is a 180-day marathon. Sometimes it takes years before students realize the impact teachers had on them. Several years after Dante, a student one of us worked with at a juvenile center, left the facility, he wrote the following letter to one of his teachers there:

Dear Ms. R,

I been meaning to write you for a long time so I could say thanks 'cause you were there for me. I got a job and a family now. My kid is 6 and he's doing good. When we were together at Craig, I couldn't really talk much back then. I was too mad at my ma who walked out on us and my dad who drank too much. I couldn't face all that stuff then, but you really listened to me. I always knew you cared. I just want you to know I'm sorry I acted like a fool sometimes.

Thanks again Ms. R.

Make Success a Daily Goal for Each Student

Students must arrive at school feeling hopeful that success will be their internal reward when they put forth reasonable effort. Acting out or giving up are the main defenses that students use to hide feelings of inadequacy when they repeatedly experience failure and don't improve. There are a number of things teachers can do to combat these feelings:

• Allow students to redo, retake, and revise tests, quizzes, and homework.

• Tell discouraged students in advance when you plan to call on them, and prepare them to answer the question correctly so they can feel good and look good in front of their peers.

• Encourage students to contribute questions for an upcoming test, and promise that at least 25 percent of the test will consist of their questions.

• Offer at least one "wild card" question on every test or assignment. That is, students can pick one question they don't want to answer. In its place, they can write another question they wish had been asked. This gesture creates student ownership and guarantees at least partial success.

• Consider making homework a bonus rather than a requirement. Doing so eliminates punishing otherwise capable students who do well on performance measures like tests without doing assignments. In fact, there is some research that suggests that homework does not improve educational outcomes and little if any that suggests it does (Maltese, Tai, & Fan, 2012).

• Allow students who do assignments to accumulate points that can be used to help increase a poor grade.

• Ask students to keep a daily journal of one new thing they learned or got better at each day. Let them know they will be successful if they follow three guidelines: (1) show up; (2) prepare, plan, practice, and persevere; and (3) focus on today. Remind them that yesterday is done and tomorrow hasn't yet arrived.

• Shut down negative thinking. Make it unacceptable to say "I can't," "I'm unable," and "It's too hard" unless adding the words "yet" or "so far."

• Emphasize that the most important thing is for each student to improve each day—not necessarily to be better than anyone or everyone else, but better than they were. Give students assignments they can handle. If they were able to write two complete sentences yesterday, try for three today. Base a significant portion of each grade on improvement rather than how each did compared with others.

• Let students know that failure often lies on the path to success. Most important, when they experience failure, show understanding and offer encouragement. For example, you might say,

> I know you are disappointed. Reading is tough for you. Certain skills are tougher for some students than for others, and that feels frustrating. I feel like giving up, too, sometimes. I had a really hard time with biology and geometry. You are smart about a lot of things, and I am going to make sure you become a better reader. You just are not allowed to quit on me! I promise not to quit on you!

• Define a mistake as a learning opportunity. For example, "I'm glad you understand how you made this mistake. This experience will help you solve this problem in the future." Here are a few examples of encouraging sentences:

> "That was a really good effort."

> "I thought your first example was really well done, even though you didn't get around to the other three."

> "This was a tough assignment, and I appreciate the effort."

> "I know this is hard, and it takes a lot of guts to try."

> "Even though your work is not complete, your effort and hard work are appreciated."

> "You are on your way. Way to go!"

> "I am proud of you."

• Base encouragement on effort, because it is the only attribute that consistently produces pride and hope. The saying that "success breeds success" is false if the success is due to cheating, questions that are too easy, or help that may not be available in the future. Easy questions that require minimal effort may be necessary initially to reawaken the feeling of success in a student who has given up, but ultimately the questions need to get harder and the effort greater in order for a "success belief" to grow.

Make Your Classroom a Motivating Place

Recently a half-page article appeared in the main section of the local newspaper about a "radical" new approach to motivating students and getting them to learn. The gist of the article was that teachers should ask students what they want to learn and create lessons related to their interests. Radical? We don't think so. We believe that although learning content is important, knowing about the interests of students and what they want to know more about is probably the best way to design lessons that get and keep students motivated. One way to quickly acquire this information is to administer a "Getting to Know You Better Inventory" (Figure 5.3).

Students often ask, "When are we ever going to use this in our lives?" When students fail to see the relevance of the content being

---

Figure 5.3
"Getting to Know You Better" Inventory

Concerning this class, I . . .

like _____.

do not like _____.

want to learn _____.

learn best when _____.

wish we could _____.

wish we didn't have to _____.

Outside of this class, I . . .

like to do _____.

am good at _____.

spend lots of time _____.

never miss the TV show _____.

am happy when _____.

wish I could _____.

---

taught to their lives, they become bored and uninterested. Students who value school because they understand a good education leads to success in life or because their parents insist on high achievement may tolerate boring classrooms. However, for those students who cannot relate future success to present-day schoolwork, it is better to connect the content with something in their current life than to connect it to a future goal. In today's fast-paced world, the future is too far away to act as a motivator. Most students live in the present—they get impatient if it takes more than a second for a website to load on their screens! Another reality that makes it even harder for students to visualize the connection between school and the future is that many of the jobs of today will cease to exist in the future.

When planning lessons with motivation in mind, remember that the first five minutes are the most important. Begin each class with an attention grabber: a great story, an existential question, a joke, an experiment, or an interesting photo. This technique is often used in the field of entertainment to keep viewers interested.

If you cannot find a way to make the lesson relevant, at least relate to your students for a few seconds every day around something you know they find interesting. Hint: music, sports, video games, and money are topics that are virtually always of interest to students. Know a little bit about a lot of things. Show your knowledge—or your ignorance. For example, "Mara, I listened to Snoop Dogg yesterday for five straight minutes! I still can't understand his message! Can you help an old guy like me understand what I'm missing?"

Finally, get your students to believe in their endless possibilities. A wonderful story in *USA Today* (Fisher, 2007) profiled Jeff Lewis, a high school math teacher in Mesa, Arizona. He taught for 28 years before contracting a blood infection that nearly killed him. As a result, Jeff became a quadruple amputee with prosthetic limbs. The story noted that he completed a 4.2-mile race, frequently goes bowling, and occasionally wears shorts to school to show what prostheses look like. The article includes quotes from his students: "He is a funny, funny man. . . . Some teachers can be sourpusses, but not Mr. Lewis. He out of all people should be, but he doesn't let difficulties get to him. . . . Mr. Lewis always makes geometry fun. You can never guess what will happen because he is so unpredictable." Lewis offers his students and others this advice: "Do not be a spectator. Life is 10 percent what happens to you and 90 percent how you respond to it."

Teach Responsibility and Caring

Discipline with Dignity emphasizes fostering critical thinking and shared decision making. Children feel affirmed without always getting their way. They understand they have some control over what happens to them, and they understand that teachers also have rights, power, knowledge, and leadership. Teachers who subscribe to the responsibility model follow this adage: "If you want true power, you must give some of it away." Students cannot learn responsibility without choices and without an opportunity to make mistakes and learn from them. The best way to promote responsibility is to involve students in as many decisions as possible. For example, "Hidalgo, talking out of turn makes it hard to give everyone a chance. We talked about this, and it is still a problem. How do you plan to solve this problem, because I prefer you handle it yourself. What consequence would be fair if you forget to follow your plan?" The following examples are strategies that teach responsibility.

Have students help one another. Create an "I'm Good At" board. Ask students to write down one or two things they believe they are good at. Younger children can draw pictures. When others have a question, concern, or problem, they can check the board to see who might be able to help before asking the teacher.

Give choices within assignments and behaviors. As we've mentioned earlier, you can get more productivity from students by offering choices in homework, tests, quizzes, and other schoolwork. For example, if you give 10 problems, ask them to choose whichever 5 best show their understanding of the material. Giving choices to students has three benefits: (1) it reduces the number of answers you have to grade; (2) some students might even do all 10 in search of the easiest, and thus gain a feeling of power and control; (3) students will at least scan all 10 questions in their minds in order to choose the 5 they will answer. Here are some other examples of ways to give students choices:

• "Answer Questions 1 to 3 in writing or create music that includes at least three of the main facts."
• "Borrow a pencil or buy one from me."
• "When people call you names, tell them you don't like it, walk away, or ask me for a suggestion."

Put students in charge of classroom responsibilities. Create a "student ambassador" program. Ambassadors welcome new students to school, give them a tour, and teach them procedures and rules. Difficult students often make the best ambassadors. Each is expected to display a high standard of performance and behavior (although not perfection). In high school, juniors and seniors can perform a similar function for first-year students. Here are a few other ways of putting students in charge:

- Noise patrol (monitors remind students in their area of the classroom to quiet down when the teacher gives a signal)
- Greeting visitors
- Supplying materials if peers forget something
- Running errands
- Helping to write test or quiz questions
- Bully lookout

Set up conference time. Provide opportunities for students to share concerns at a time of relative convenience. For example, "On Friday morning from 11 to 11:45 a.m., we will be doing a cooperative learning activity. During that time, any of you can sign up for five minutes to privately talk with me, complain, share a suggestion, or disagree about anything you want." When students take you up on your offer, listen closely and take notes. When appropriate, tell the entire class what you learned and plan to do differently. For example, "Many of you say I am not returning feedback and grades quickly enough. I think you are right. I can't promise it will always happen, but I will do my best to return assignments within three days of your handing them in."

Establish Formal Discipline Procedures

The best way to create formal discipline procedures is to make sure all values, rules, and consequences are clearly understood, are predictable, and include student input. We call this process a "social contract" and describe it in detail in the next chapter.

6

Formal Discipline: The Social Contract

In theory, schools are laboratories that children enter at age 5 and adults exit at age 18. This process of maturation has two significant parts. The first is to acquire skills, knowledge, and understandings to prepare for work and advanced schooling and to be informed citizens. The second part is to become socialized by learning how to interact with others, resolve conflicts, share, and make good decisions.

Society expresses strong differences of opinion as to which of these two goals is the higher priority. We believe both are highly important and are, in fact, intertwined. When taught correctly, academic subjects inform the socialization process, just as learning social skills helps students learn academics.

Many teachers define *discipline* as correcting behavior problems. We believe that discipline is the heart of the socialization process. All of the social skills students learn are related to discipline in one way or another. When discipline is used to teach instead of to threaten, punish, and reward, students have the opportunity to learn the critical social skills necessary for responsible adulthood.

Formal Versus Informal Discipline Systems

Social skills can be taught through two systems: formal and informal. In the best schools, these systems support each other and teach the same skills in different ways. In less effective schools, these systems work against each other.

The Formal System

The formal system consists of three parts: values, rules/expectations, and consequences. Formal discipline is usually codified by the school and published in a handbook, a code of conduct, or a parent handbook or communicated via another formal mechanism.

Values are expressed in the vision, mission, and moral code of the school. They provide the foundation for *why* we expect students to behave in certain ways. To be enforced, values require clearly defined rules and consequences. Some educators prefer the term *expectations* to *rules* because of its more positive connotation. They view *expectations* in terms of what students *should* do, versus *rules*, which refer to what students *should not* do. We use these terms interchangeably, because we believe they can be framed in terms of either or both meanings.

Rules identify *how* students are or are not expected to act. At a minimum, schoolwide rules cover major infractions that are in direct opposition to accepted values; these include fighting, getting high on school grounds, and vandalism. Violations of such rules become part of a student's record. Such rules may also address behaviors in the hallways, in the cafeteria, and during recess. Classroom rules identify key behaviors and procedures that are opposed to classroom values and often are required for effective teaching and learning to occur. All behaviors related to safety need to be addressed formally, as do those that predictably interfere with teaching and learning.

All rules must be enforced because otherwise the values of the school will be violated with impunity. We recommend that threats, punishments, and a structured system of rewards be used only in a very limited manner. Consequences in school, unlike punishments that rely principally on fear and misery, should be designed to teach students to make better choices.

Rules should be reserved for behaviors that are harmful and those that significantly impede teaching or learning. It is impossible to have rules for everything. Schools and teachers that try to cover all behaviors with formal rules and consequences can easily get bogged down with a long list that makes well-behaved students feel like they're in prison and gives poorly behaving students ideas for disrupting that they hadn't thought of previously. Long lists of rules are also difficult for the teacher to enforce with a formal consequence.

The Informal System

The informal system includes two parts: interruptions and interventions. A number of student behaviors are considered inappropriate, ranging from trivial silliness to more disruptive intrusions like burping, humming, talking out of turn, and others too numerous to list. Infrequent or less formalized disruptions may be called by many names, including "procedure violations" or "minor infractions." We choose to call them *behavioral interruptions*. The name is less important than the concept. Teachers can usually address these interruptions quickly and informally with actions such as looking a student in the eye or telling a student to "stop" so the lesson can resume (see Chapter 8 on interrupting misbehavior with good teaching). However, even these minor violations may need formal rules and consequences if they happen often and consume excessive instructional time. That is a judgment call to be made by the teacher or perhaps the students, based on instructional goals and teaching style.

The Social Contract: Values, Rules, and Consequences

Troubled schools are those with rules that go unenforced and consequences that cause more behavior problems in the future by not addressing the real reasons for the misbehavior. We believe it helps to have a structure guiding teachers and students that includes values, rules, and consequences all working together. We call this a *social contract*. It is essentially an agreement between teacher and students about the values, rules, and consequences for behavior.

Keys to an Effective Social Contract

The keys to developing an effective social contract are the following:

- Identify the values of the classroom.
- Identify rules needed to run an effective classroom.
- Connect rules/expectations to values.
- Involve students in helping to develop rules for what they need from you and each other for success.
- Ensure that rules are clear and specific.
- Relate consequences to the rule as directly as possible.
- Ensure that consequences are always guided by the goal of learning and improved behavior, not by creating misery.
- Develop a range of consequences for rule violations, with at least three options.
- If a student or parent thinks a different consequence will be more effective to change behavior, consider accepting the alternative, but ask what should happen if there is no improvement.
- Ensure that learning to make good choices, rather than political correctness, guides the use of rules and consequences.
- Review and update the contract regularly (we suggest once per month), or more often if necessary.

The Relationship Between Rules and Values/Principles

When you board an airplane, the first thing the flight attendant usually says is "Your safety is our number-one priority, so please listen carefully to these important instructions for the next few moments." Safety is a *value*, not a *rule*. Safety is too vague to be a rule. Three actual, enforceable rules related to safety on an airplane are "Fasten your seatbelts. Shut off all electronic devices. Set tray tables and seatbacks in the upright position." These rules tell us what to do.

When we understand why we are expected to follow certain rules, we become more motivated to follow them. Values provide the rationale for rules. Here are the most important values that every school must have:

- Everyone has a right to feel safe at school, on the bus, and online.
- All students have a right to learn without bothering or being bothered by others.
- Everyone in the school is expected to learn.

Here are other values a school might include:

- Be helpful.
- Respect this place, yourself, and one another.
- Be responsible for yourself.
- Care about others.
- Treat others with dignity.
- Take pride in accomplishments.
- Honor differences rather than mock them.

After carefully identifying and explaining the need for the values, teachers can invite students to help formulate other values that matter to them and then to participate in developing rules. Figure 6.1 shows an example of values and corresponding rules.

Figure 6.1
Mrs. Connor's Class Values and Rules

Value: I have a right to be happy and to be treated with kindness and dignity in this room.
Rule: This means no one will laugh at me, ignore me, or hurt my feelings.

Value: I have a right to be myself in this room.
Rule: This means that no one will treat me unfairly because I am overweight or thin, fast or slow, boy or girl.

Value: I have a right to feel safe in this room.
Rule: This means that no one will hit, kick, push, or pinch.

Value: I have a right to learn about myself in this room.
Rule: This means I am free to speak at an appropriate time without being interrupted or punished.

Developing Effective Rules

As we have explained, rules are guidelines for specific actions and behaviors based on values. They define *what* is acceptable and what is not. They also define *how* students and staff are expected to behave. A good rule has three attributes: it should be (1) easy to remember, (2) precise, and, when possible, (3) focused more on the positive than the negative.

Easy to remember. Here's an example of a rule that's too long and complicated: "Because there are so many students in class and the room is small and desks are too close together, everyone must sit down when the first bell rings unless you have the teacher's permission to stand." Here's a preferable substitute: "Because we value safety, please sit when the first bell rings." The first example provides a good explanation of the rationale for the rule, and a teacher could use it if students asked about the need for the rule.

Precise. A good rule allows for no debate or gray areas when someone argues or objects. "The speed limit is 40. You are going 50. You are speeding." However, it is possible to make rules either too specific or too vague. Here are examples of rules that are too specific or too vague, as well as proper revisions:

Too vague: Each student must not interfere with another student's learning. (This statement would be a fine *value,* not a *rule.*)

Too specific: Do not poke your fingers in another student's eye.

Just right: People are not for hitting. Keep hands and feet to yourself.

Too vague: Do not stop others from learning.

Too specific: Never talk when others are talking.

Just right: Raise hands in class discussions before contributing.

Focused more on the positive than the negative, when possible. For example, "Be on time" is preferable to "Don't be late." Some rules, however, like "no insults allowed," have no positive expression and are therefore acceptable.

Rules are important communication tools for parents and the community at large. In the rare cases of legal issues, the clarity and quality of rules can protect the school and the administration when dealing with lawyers. Thus, all classroom and school rules and consequences should be shared across the school community.

Types of Rules

Generally, we can categorize rules into five types, each with its own set of concerns:

• *Academic rules* are those related to learning, such as doing homework, class participation, cheating, and interrupting others.

• *Social rules* are those that involve how to act toward others, such as how to have a conversation, express feelings, take turns, collaborate, and respectfully disagree.

• *Procedural rules* affect such issues as being on time, lining up, getting notes from home when necessary, dress codes (if your school has them), entering and exiting the classroom, participating in class discussions, turning in papers, what to do if students forget to bring materials, and the proper use of technology-related devices.

• *Cultural rules* are about the way we treat minority groups, including those based on religion, race, sexual orientation, or disability.

• *Safety rules* are concerned with making the school safe and secure and address such issues as weapons in school, wearing gang colors, bullying, and, for younger students, running in the hall.

These categories are not absolute and are simply meant to be guidelines in developing rules, adding some clarity when thinking about the issues facing your school. Worry less about deciding which is the best category for a rule and more about making rules effective.

How to Develop Schoolwide Rules

Schoolwide rules are important in common areas like hallways, lunchrooms, and libraries. Here are specific steps for creating good schoolwide rules:

1. Explain the difference between rules and values to faculty.

2. Post school values as defined by the school board or administration. In rare cases where no defined values exist, consider developing some in categories such as academic, social, procedural, cultural, and safety. Discussing the school's mission can also lead the way in defining its values.

3. Teachers and administrators discuss and create lists of specific rules and expectations directly related to each value, incorporating, where appropriate, ideas generated by students (see next section for more on student involvement).

4. Privately vote on each, with 75 percent agreement needed for acceptance.

5. Determine a final list of school rules and expectations.

This process may take a while to complete, because each step requires a certain amount of energy and time, and strong debate may take place. Dividing into various work groups at various stages of the process can be helpful.

Student Involvement in Developing Rules

From its inception, a unique aspect of Discipline with Dignity has been its active involvement of students in developing the rules they are expected to follow. Students are more likely to follow rules if they have a say in what those rules are. They don't need to have a say in every rule, nor should they establish rules that are contrary to school values, procedures, or functions. However, listening to all their ideas, whether accepted or not, can be very helpful in meeting their needs. In actuality, we have found that when students and teachers are separately asked to identify rules that they think are necessary, there is a greater than 90 percent agreement between the groups. It is really the *perception of ownership* that makes students feel empowered and respected. You can begin by asking students what kind of classroom they want to have that will make them feel safe and help them learn. List the ideas and see how they fit with yours. From that list and any others the class might brainstorm, the rules are developed, and if necessary, the teacher explains how they may differ from "behavioral interruptions."

The issue of personal safety is one where student involvement is especially important. To a large extent, we must depend on students to help make and keep the school safe for everyone. Emphasize the importance of "If you see something, say something." Students are usually the first to hear about and to have to deal with dangerous situations, like cyber-bullying, that happen when adults are not around. Be sure students have safe, secure ways to report inappropriate behavior without fear of repercussion. If they are concerned about directly telling an adult, be sure to have alternatives like an emergency in-school hotline, a "serious concern" reporting box, or a social media vehicle. Some "must report to adult" behaviors include the following:

- Illegal behavior such as selling drugs or stealing
- Posting hurtful pictures, tweets, or texts
- Bringing or talking about bringing a weapon to school
- Planning to cause harm to other people or property at school or outside school

There are various ways to involve students in the process of developing rules related to personal safety. Here are some suggestions:

- Have each class form a committee to develop strategies. Be sure to include students who have had behavior problems in the past; they will often give the best suggestions when put in charge.
- Have students create posters on these topics displayed throughout the school.
- Ask students to develop and perform advertisements for "see it, say it" behavior.
- Allow students to teach social media etiquette and to involve and inform parents.

As a last step in the overall rule-developing process, ask students to create rules for the teacher. This is best done in small groups.

Accept at least one or two rules to show that you care what students think. Do not accept a rule or consequence you can't live with. Typical examples of rules for teachers include the following:

- Return homework within three days of it being turned in.
- If students must say "please" and "thank you," so must the teacher.
- The teacher must be on time and ready to begin teaching when the bell rings.
- If students can't eat in class (or chew gum or drink), neither should the teacher.
- Say hello to students in a friendly way when they enter the classroom.

After the schoolwide values and rules are developed, it is advisable to let parents know the specifics. Involving parents makes them more likely to help their children honor all the rules. Send a copy of the values and rules home, text them, and use your class Facebook page or school website to explain that the rules were developed with the involvement of their children. Ask for their input, including any rules they value that may have been omitted. You can also use a parent night to share, reinforce, and seek this information.

Understanding Consequences and How They Differ from Punishments

The classical definition of a *consequence* is "what we do to ourselves." Consequences are the result of our own choices. If we are late to the airport, we miss our flight. If we don't charge our cell phones, the battery dies. If we yell at our students enough, they stop listening. The most effective consequences usually relate as directly to the rule as possible: If you make a mess, you must clean it up. If you do something destructive, you must do something constructive.

A consequence is merely a vehicle to a destination. When teachers are frustrated, it is understandable that they may want misery for the student and forget that the goal is for the student to make better choices. Consequences should therefore involve the student, and they can be negotiable; but the destination (appropriate behavior) is not negotiable. For example, if a student hits in anger, not hitting when angry is the destination. The vehicle can be a phone call home, a five-minute conversation after class, an hour of practice at school, or something created by the student or teacher. Because consequences are the result of choices, they involve student action. Consequences are what students do. All consequences involve the student improving behavior by doing something. The teacher may initiate the student action—for example, by asking a student to help another student—but the student does the helping.

Although outcome is most important in deciding whether to use or continue using a particular consequence, it is essential that the consequence avoid humiliation. Be careful not to confuse consequences with punishments. Punishments, unlike consequences, are done *to* the student, not to *help* the student. Punishments are intended to inflict misery. A common belief is that pain will get people to avoid doing what got them into trouble. In reality, when dealing with the most difficult students, it is impossible to punish them more than life itself already has, which is why punishment is so rarely effective. A punishment has the following characteristics:

- It has no relation to the rule.
- It typically humiliates the student.
- It is derived from a threat and deters future negative behavior out of fear.
- It involves little choice for students.
- It focuses on what has happened, not what will happen.
- It hinders motivation to learn.
- It hinders the development of responsibility and increased obedience.

A helpful way to decide if an intervention is a punishment or a consequence is to put ourselves at the receiving end and consider what our own reaction would be.

Including Students in Developing Consequences

Many educators are reluctant to involve students in the process of developing consequences. When the first edition of this book was published, we were too. We advocated having students create rules, but not consequences. Our view has changed. Students are capable of having a say in consequences as well as rules. Here is an example of a student creating a consequence:

Student: I do not want to stay after school to develop a behavior plan with you.

Teacher: I am so frustrated with your talking, and I don't know what else to do. So if you have a better solution, tell me what it is. If you were me, what would you do?

Student: Probably I'd move my seat.

Teacher: How would that help?

Student: The two girls I sit by in your class are always talking to me, and they make me laugh. I guess they also think I'm funny. They're kind of friends with me, so if you move my seat, I won't feel like I have to entertain them.

Teacher: Where is a good place for you to move that will solve the problem?

Student: Right in front of you.

Teacher: Sounds good. Let's meet again at the end of the week to see how things are going.

Remember, the outcome of the consequence is to learn improved behavior that lasts. If a student believes that something else will work better, go along if the idea seems sensible. Let the student prove to himself and to you that he has what it takes before you become more insistent. What matters most is not the specific consequence, but having the student learn a more acceptable and productive way to behave. If students think they have a better way to improve in any aspect of school, encourage them to express their ideas. Doing so teaches them responsibility. Consider the following example:

> *Student:* I do not think that I should have to do 10 problems!
>
> *Teacher:* OK, why not?
>
> *Student:* Because it will only take me 5 to show you I know how to multiply.
>
> *Teacher:* Perfect. I look forward to seeing 5 problems tomorrow. By the way, if you don't complete 5, what do you think should happen?

Why Sequenced Consequences Are a Bad Idea

Sequenced consequences or punishments are usually numbered one through five and are presented in a specific order. For example, notice how these punishments are ordered:

> *First offense:* Warning
>
> *Second offense:* Phone call home
>
> *Third offense:* Discussion with teacher, detention
>
> *Fourth offense:* In-school suspension, meeting with counselor
>
> *Fifth offense:* Out-of-school suspension

Instead of sequencing, tell students something like this: "These are some potential consequences when you break a rule. One of these might happen, but there is no predetermined order. Or none of these might happen, because I always reserve the right to go off the list. We will pick the most appropriate consequence based on what will help each individual."

Sequencing consequences forces us to do things that might not work. For example, for some children, parents are a source of the problem; in other cases, the student has already convinced the parents that the teacher is at fault. In either scenario, calling home is a waste of time. Other students may love detention because a safe, structured environment is a rarity for them.

The main thing to keep in mind about consequences is that they should be simultaneously *predictable* and *flexible*.

Why "Fair" Does Not Always Mean "Equal"

It is a mistake to believe that if Violet and Jen break the same rule, they must get the same consequence. It is extremely important to teach and explain to your students that "fair" and "equal" can but do not have to mean the same thing (Mendler, Curwin, & Mendler, 2008). If a student complains about another student's consequence, test, quiz, or homework assignment, you can invite alternatives, but do not discuss the other student. Consider this example:

> *Violet:* You are making me stay after school and only calling Jen's mom. That's not fair!
>
> *Teacher:* Violet, what's the problem with the consequence I gave you?
>
> *Violet:* But Jen got . . .
>
> *Teacher (cutting Violet off):* I know what Jen got, but I am not talking about her. What's the problem with what I did for you?
>
> *Violet:* But Jen did the same . . .
>
> *Teacher:* I know, and that's between Jen and me. When you are ready to talk about Violet, I am glad to listen. Take a little time and let me know if you want to talk about you—and I will never talk to Jen or anyone else about you.

In school, the word *fair* should be defined as "Each student gets what he or she needs to be successful and act in a more responsible way." Let your students know that your goal each day is for each of them to get better today—in either behavior or subject-matter learning—than they were yesterday, and not necessarily better than everybody else. Tell your students something like this:

> In our class, I will do my best to give each of you what I think you need without comparing you to each other. Although I might use the same test, quiz, homework assignment, or consequence, I won't if I think something else will help someone be more successful or better at following the rules. For example, if Stefan and Henry break the same

rule, they might get different consequences if I think they need different things to help them not make the same mistake. So if you get a consequence from me but you think there is a better one that will help you behave better, let me know in a respectful way, and I will be happy to consider it. But please don't expect me to talk to you about somebody else, because I will only listen to how you think something else will work better for you.

In actual practice, although we may use the same teaching or discipline method for most students, we'll need other methods for some, and we may need to create a new one for a particularly unique learner. This concept gives us the ability and structure to work with each student at his or her level without being influenced by what the others think.

If a parent or student complains about fairness, try using a version of the following:

To a parent: "I'm willing to consider any suggestion you have, but I'll only treat your child like everyone else if that's what helps him learn improved behavior. Because not all students learn the same way, I want to do what I think is best for him. Wouldn't you agree he deserves that?"

To a student: "I'll never discuss what happens between another student and me with you; and because I respect your dignity, I'll never discuss you with another student."

If students are still confused or if you need to reinforce the "fair is not equal" concept, you might ask them the following questions:

"Is it fair to expect a wheelchair-bound student to shower after physical education class without a special-needs shower?"

"Is it fair to ask hearing-impaired students to watch an uncaptioned video?"

"Is it fair to give the same Spanish test to a native of Mexico and a student who has never spoken the language?"

Ask students to think of other examples of fair not necessarily meaning equal. Here are some starters:

"Is it fair that in baseball, closers are paid a lot of money to pitch one inning and shortstops play nine? Often the pitcher makes *more* money than the shortstop." (fair but definitely not equal)

"Is it fair that children of different ages have different chores at home?" (fair but not equal)

"Is it fair that some children wear glasses and others do not?" (fair but not equal)

Notice the absurdity in the following example:

Judge: In all my years on the bench, I have never seen a more despicable criminal. You robbed, assaulted, and tortured the victim because he bumped you! Do you have something to say before I sentence you?

Criminal: Nope.

Judge: In that case, I hereby sentence you to 40 years in a maximum-security prison. I also sentence the victim to 40 years in prison.

Victim: Wait—what? That doesn't make any sense! He attacked me.

Judge: I don't care who started it. (Rich, 2007, p. 26)

The lesson here is simple: When it comes to people-to-people relationships, conflicts, and solutions, one size almost never fits all.

Types of Effective Consequences

Although being uncomfortable and unhappy can be and often is a by-product of a consequence, once again, becoming more responsible by making better choices is the primary goal. There are at least eight types of consequences that can be used to make that happen. Notice that the teacher instigates them, but the student does the action:

• **Consequences that are altruistic.** These involve the student doing something positive for another. Altruism is a

consequence and a healer. In cases of trauma, including returning soldiers with PTSD, cancer survivors, or victims of natural
disasters, helping others can be therapeutic. This approach works
for children with social problems in school. Here's an example:
"Pushing Samantha to be first in line was hurtful. Please think
about something nice you can do for her and tell me before lunch."

• **Consequences that teach.** If a student doesn't know how
to do something, you can't persuade or punish him to change. He
must first learn and then practice the skill. Here's an example:
"Let's practice calmly walking into class with voices lowered until
we get it right."

• **Consequences that offer choices.** These offer students
choice without threatening. Here's an example: "There are at least
three ways to avoid unpleasant confrontations: walk away, say you
see their point and respectfully disagree (or agree just to be done
with it), or make it clear you will not engage in nasty talk. But
if you are upset, I'll be glad to hear about your problem. Which
works best for you?"

• **Consequences that transform punishments.** Some
school punishments, such as referrals or calls home, can be modified to become consequences that work more effectively. Rather
than eliminate punishments, they can be changed to meet the
criteria for consequences. For example, a more effective use of
detention would be to have the teacher who assigns the detention
stay with the student and discuss why the student is there, practice
with the student, or teach new skills. To make out-of-classroom
referrals more effective, you can send the student to another
teacher, a social worker, or a counselor. Here's an example: "Kelly,
we are headed for a major disagreement. Please take a break in Mrs.
Prague's class and come back when you are ready to learn. Please do
not be too long. This lesson is too important for you to miss, and we
will miss you."

• **Consequences that inspire.** These consequences offer
hope and inspiration to change a student's attitude. Find community members who are recovered drug users or alcoholics, ex-gang
members, or prisoners. Invite them to talk with your class or a

specific student on a dangerous path. Doing so can help both the student and the community member.

• **Consequences that plan.** These consequences help students learn new responses to resolve problems. Be sure each step of the plan is behavioral and specific, not fuzzy. Here's a bad example: "So what's your plan to not yell if Casey keeps 'looking' at you?" Here's a good example: "What specifically will you do first if Casey looks at you again? What will you do next?" Be sure to help students create a plan if theirs is not complete.

• **Consequences that are based on logic.** These consequences are directly connected to a specific rule. They involve teacher intervention but still differ from punishments. They are future based and teach new behavior. Here's an example: "The cafeteria is a mess, and Mr. Custodian could use your help with the cleaning."

• **Consequences that involve parents.** These consequences create a team between home and school to help a child. Be careful not to blame parents for their child's behavior or threaten with punishment. Begin by listening and asking questions. Try not to interrogate. Find common ground before finding solutions. Here's an example: "Thank you for coming to discuss your daughter. I think she is hurting her future in school, and I hope we can find a way to help her together. Can you tell me how she behaves at home?"

Restorative Justice

Those familiar with restorative justice will see how many of its principles and practices related to consequences are embedded within our approach. For example, Holtham (2009) suggests that a restorative practice for graffiti or property damage is to have the person help clean, repair, repaint, and pay for damages. Ridicule or use of racial or ethnic slurs might require participation in a blanket drive for the homeless or organizing a panel of speakers who can talk to the entire class or school about intolerance, along with a letter of apology to the person harmed. The Center for Restorative Approaches in New Orleans claims that since January 2015, restorative justice circles, in which students and staff talk through the root causes of conflict in the classroom, have saved the city's students 1,800 instructional hours (Shaw, 2016). A Virginia judge recently ordered five vandals to each read one book a month for 12 months, choosing from among 35 titles pertaining to acts of hatred, and to write a book report as a punishment for covering a historic black schoolhouse with racist, obscene, and anti-Semitic graffiti. The teens were also required to watch 14 films; visit two museums, including the U.S. Holocaust Museum; and write a report on the effects of hate within the community (Hauser, 2017). All of these actions, like the consequences suggested within Discipline with Dignity, are about teaching improved behavior to prevent a recurrence of the problem and, to the degree possible, repairing whatever physical or emotional damage was done.

The "How" Is More Important Than the "What"

The way we implement a consequence is often more important than the consequence itself in determining effectiveness. It is best to put yourself at the receiving end of a consequence and ask yourself whether your dignity would be preserved or attacked. Consequences are best delivered calmly, privately, and with the utmost dignity.

Be Aware of the System Effect

As we have noted, the social contract is a system of values, rules, and consequences. Although systems are necessary to provide structure and guidelines, we must never feel enslaved by them. Systems should exist to serve people rather than requiring that people always fit the system. Two attitudes make sure the social contract system serves students effectively:

• Instead of saying, "If I do it for you, I'll have to do it for everyone," try "Let me see if I can make this work for you without making everyone else unhappy."
• Instead of saying, "This is the system we use, and there is nothing I can do about it," try "This is our system. How can we tweak it for you?"

Students can become cynical, unmotivated, alienated, or hostile if they perceive the system doesn't care about them. They will often take out their frustrations, either actively or passive-aggressively, by striking back at those who created the system. Such students feel gratified by beating the system—or even attempting to. In their mind, the reasons and rationality for maintaining order become meaningless.

Systems are not intended to be malicious. The way people use them determines whether they are helpful or a roadblock to human interaction.

When students see that the classroom values efficiency over humanity, many will disrupt it. When they perceive the classroom as the corner store, they feel welcome and valued. Nearly every school has a few teachers who have earned respect from the toughest students. When asked why they like these teachers, the students say, "He treats me as a human"; "She treats me with respect"; "He cares about me as a person, not just as a student"; "She listens"; "He doesn't tell me what to do all the time"; "She gives me the chance to make my own decisions"; and "He believes in me—he believes I can succeed." These teachers have systems that guide instead of control what they and their students do.

The social contract is a system designed to enhance human interaction in the classroom. The process includes shared decision making, opportunity for change, and the chance to see situations for all their natural complexity rather than simplify them down to "easily manageable levels." This approach also builds potential for inefficiency and human mistakes, but in the long run, working through problem situations rather than letting a system make the decision enhances the classroom environment.

7

Taking Action:
The Informal Discipline System

In the previous chapter we explained how to improve the formal discipline process of classrooms and schools. But schools also operate informal systems to deal with minor infractions of rules, which are more frequent than violations of the formal system. We call these less serious violations *behavioral interruptions*. Here are some examples:

- Talking when another student is talking
- Not sitting when asked
- Slamming a door
- Using an unauthorized electronic device
- Disrupting the lesson by humming, tapping, and so on
- Not doing homework or in-class assignments
- Engaging in horseplay
- Throwing harmless objects

Behaviors like these still need to be addressed if they have not been incorporated into rules. In these cases, it is best to use interventions other than consequences. Whereas consequences are formal responses to a specific rule violation, informal interventions have two primary goals: (1) get the behavior to quickly slow down or stop, and (2) get back to teaching. Sometimes a behavioral interruption can develop into a more serious problem that should be incorporated into a rule. For example, using a smartphone might be considered an interruption, but if it happens often enough, you might want to develop a rule governing its use.

Assessing the Problem to Choose the Best Intervention

Teachers frequently ask us, "When my student does [misbehavior], what should I do?" The following are questions and suggestions to help figure out answers.

What did you try before when this happened? Did it ever help? Were there any unintended negative results? Keep in mind the five-trial/two- to three-week guideline, since change is usually a roller coaster (see p. 53). Even when a strategy is already working, a student may revisit her old behaviors. Such relapses often lead to teacher discouragement, so be sure to get past those feelings before you decide whether to persevere with the strategy or let it go.

Which is more important to you—that the student feel bad about what he did or that he change his behavior? Although regret or remorse is often a necessary first step leading to change, sometimes the intervention makes a student feel bad but he still repeats the behavior—often because he feels bad about what happens to him rather than what he has done. As well, in some cases an intervention does not make the student feel bad but nevertheless stops the behavior. The best interventions trigger feelings of remorse and regret that lead to change and improvement.

What haven't you tried that might work? Let's consider this question in the context of teacher anger. Unlike a car, anger is not shut off with the push of a button or turn of a key. If we are usually angry, students stop taking us seriously. Consider the following example. A student calls her classmate a very hurtful name, offending the teacher, who is shocked to hear such language coming from that student's mouth. In the past when this has happened with other students, the teacher reacted by yelling and demanding that they never use those words again. Given the student's use of the same words, this past intervention obviously hasn't worked. The teacher may have gotten better results had she first taken a few deep breaths to calm herself, perhaps shown empathy (e.g., "Using those words tells me you are very angry"), deferred to explore more fully ("After class I want to hear more about it"), offered a quick alternative ("How about counting or taking a few deep breaths?"), and ended by getting back to the lesson ("Thanks for calming yourself and agreeing to tell me more later"). It is useful to review every situation after the fact to pinpoint what went well and what needs improving. Choosing an ineffective method of dealing with your student is not a mistake if it helps you learn new options.

In addition to the "What should I do?" question, teachers also often ask us, "If it didn't work, should I do the same thing again?" If the strategy seems sensible and the potential benefits outweigh the risks, do a selected intervention at least five times or for a period of two or three weeks to decide if it works.

Turning Teacher Anger into a Helpful Example

As illustrated by the example we just shared, interventions usually work best when expressed in a controlled and calm way. We must filter our emotions so that anger doesn't dominate. Yet feeling angry is natural. In many ways, students can actually benefit from seeing us angry because it can help them understand that their behavior is entirely unacceptable and that anger is often a natural consequence of doing hurtful things.

It is also important for students to see how anger does not have to lead to escalation. Show students a healthy way to express anger. For example, you might say, "Your words are unacceptable even if you are angry! Right now, I feel like saying hurtful things to you, but instead I'm going to walk away, take a few breaths, calm down, and think about what I want to do next."

Our students are likely to see anger throughout their lives. As adults, they may experience it from spouses, bosses, fellow workers, and their own children. Show them that anger can be expressed without escalating a conflict.

Interventions for Classroom Misbehavior

As we explained in the last chapter, teachers usually initiate consequences for violations of rules, but students—to learn and practice
making better choices—do the primary work. On the other hand,
interventions for behavioral interruptions require little or no action
by the student. The following interventions are often very effective at stopping misbehavior and de-escalating conflict at the same
time. Their purpose is to keep students in class, get back to teaching,
and, if necessary, postpone using other interventions that take more
time.

The Two-Step Intervention

The two-step intervention is derived from the procedure that first
responders use in emergency situations. Think of a hospital emergency room. The first priority of staff is to stabilize the patient and
then either admit him to the hospital or arrange outpatient treatment.
The goal is to stop patients from getting worse. The same is true for
firefighters, police officers, soldiers, and all other first responders.
They stabilize first and repair second.

The two-step intervention for students uses the same process.
First, stabilize to calm the student and the situation. Second, repair
the damage that was created.

Most students can be taught to stabilize themselves by taking
extra-deep breaths when they are upset or using similar easy-to-learn
strategies (see Chapter 10). Many of us have angrily written e-mails
and posted to social media and then, upon reflection, wished we had
never clicked "Send." The time to resolve an issue or seek a long-term
solution is after anger subsides. Otherwise situations usually worsen,
other people often get involved, things are said or done that are hard
to take back, and a great deal of time is wasted.

If stabilization techniques such as taking deep breaths are not
followed by a resolution strategy, they will not solve the problem. Visualize the resolution strategy you might try when things calm down.
The following are some examples and points to keep in mind.

- **Understand that stabilizing is not excusing.** It is simply deferring the resolution to a more favorable time; for example, "I can see you are super-upset, but right now neither of us can fix this. Thanks so much for waiting until after class."
- **Show students you are willing to listen to their side of the story.** For example, after being corrected, a student says about another, "She started it" or "He's lying." You can respond by saying, "I'm sure you have your reasons for hitting, but hitting is not acceptable. After class I want to hear reasons so we can figure out better ways to defend yourself."
- **Guess the motive for misbehavior**, and acknowledge it without agreeing to the student's choice of solution. For example, "It seems like you really want us to notice you right now. I like attention, too. As soon as I am finished reading, you can ask a question. Thank you for waiting."
- **Deflect arguing by agreeing.** If a student says, "Your lesson is so boring!" you can respond by saying, "I am sorry you feel that way, and you might be right. Can you please tell me two specific ways to make it better after the lesson?"
- **Respond unexpectedly.** We know a teacher who had a student who called her an "anorexic whore." She stopped on the spot, called her husband, and told him, "Anthony thinks I'm skinny! It's about time someone in my life complimented me!"
- **Try hard not to criticize, lecture, scold, blame, and argue.** If a student says, "I hate you!" you can respond by saying, "I am very sorry. I'm guessing it's about something I said or did that you strongly dislike. After calming down, tell me how I can be a better teacher for you."
- **Avoid embarrassing or attacking a student's dignity.** Remember the audience plays a role in every performance you see. Embarrassing students in front of their friends is never a good idea. Talk to students privately. Whisper in their ear. Use notes, laminated cards, or hand signals. When correcting a student, briefly pause and put yourself at the receiving end of what you are about to say. If it would embarrass you, it will probably embarrass

him. Forgive yourself for not being perfect and then find a time to genuinely apologize.

These stabilizers work only when they are sincere. Each of us has to find our own comfortable voice and to mean what we say. As in the emergency room, many problems can be treated or resolved on the spot. For those that can't, stabilize before resolving.

Privacy

It is always preferable to correct a student in private; however, it's not always possible. As noted earlier, discussing a behavior problem in front of others may be humiliating, even if you don't intend it to be. Reprimanding in front of others may result in a passive-aggressive episode or direct aggression either immediately or later. Sometimes a private conversation isn't possible, so be careful with your words and tone of voice. If you must correct publicly, try speaking with conviction to the child's strengths. For example, "Chris, you are a leader, and we could all get through this lesson a lot faster if you decide to cooperate!" Yell only when safety is an issue or it is absolutely necessary to be heard. Keep in mind that tough students often want to feel in charge and can be helpful when asked to exert their influence in positive ways. Focus on them. Build relationships with them. You need them more than they need you—especially if the class is chaotic. The distraction intervention described later in this chapter can help you find a private time in the middle of an ongoing class.

Eye Contact

Our eyes have power. Looking someone in the eye shows you are listening, that you care, and that you mean what you say. However, in some cultures children are taught that it is disrespectful to look an adult in the eyes. If doing so is not a taboo for your student, use your eyes when discussing behavior issues. Lock your eyes on theirs. If they look away, stop talking until they look back, and maintain eye contact for three to five seconds after you have delivered your message.

Looking your student in the eyes is more powerful than yelling or sounding tough. You can get your message across without sounding angry or hostile. If your student won't look into your eyes, then increase eye contact gradually. Never make eye contact an issue on top of the original one. Avoid saying "Look at me when I talk to you," because now you are shifting the focus of the intervention away from the original problem.

Proximity

Proximity is how close you are when you talk to a student. It provides opportunities to deliver a powerful message without yelling or expressing anger. The powerful combination of privacy, eye contact, and proximity can resolve most problems without further intervention. Imagine talking privately, looking a student in the eyes when appropriate, and then inching closer while remaining calm, firm, and free of emotion: "Thank you for not shoving other people even when angry."

You can use your instincts to determine optimal proximity when delivering a message, but it's helpful to know that the distance between you and your student will vary based on age, grade, the relationship you have built (the stronger the relationship, the closer you can usually get), and cultural considerations. In terms of age and grade, here are some general guidelines:

- Teenagers: one step closer than arm's-length
- Preteens (6–12): two steps closer than arm's-length
- Youngsters (4–6): one foot from their eyes
- Toddlers (2–4): eye to eye

With older students in particular, you don't want to "invade their space" in a negative way. You don't want to hear "Get outta my face!" as their response, but if that is what you get, take a step or two back and say, "Is this better?" and then get back to the lesson.

Don't argue over who gets the "last word." With difficult students, be satisfied with the most effective word, which often comes "next to last." Let the student get the last word. He needs it to save face with the people he eats lunch with and rides the bus with.

As with eye contact, people of different cultures have different reactions to closeness. For example, in some Eastern cultures, people stand further away from each other when communicating. In most Western cultures, a comfortable conversational distance is arm's-length away.

Remember that what we offer here are guidelines and suggestions. Again, trust your instincts, recognizing that there is no substitute for knowing each student. If a student seems intimidated, back off. Some might be frightened and even cry the first few times you approach them closely. With a hand on the student's shoulder, keep eye contact and remind him you care about and believe in him. Tell him it's OK to cry. Say, "When I get upset, I cry, too, sometimes."

Recognizing that some teachers are more comfortable than others in terms of proximity, we suggest approaching the edge of your comfort zone when using it. Continually adjust until you have figured out what is best for each student.

A final way to use proximity is simply to stand or sit as close as possible to a student when she is doing something inappropriate. Say nothing. Rely on physical presence alone to send the message.

Distraction

If class time is limited and you want a more extensive discussion with a student about her behavior, you can talk privately during class without losing instructional time. Do so in the context of group or partner work or individual assignments that allow students to consult with each other. While others are "distracted" by the assignment (ideally on a topic that is likely to grab their attention), talk with the individual student. Most of the others won't notice.

It is also wise to tell students early in the year that you will frequently have private individual conversations with them during class time because that is your way of giving them feedback. Assure them that you will not be sharing the conversations with anyone else. Preparing students this way helps them understand that your private chats are a natural part of the classroom experience, and they will likely stop asking what you are doing.

Sometimes it's difficult to think of a good distracting activity in the moment. Until this practice becomes easier, preplan a few distracting activities. Each distraction should have two characteristics. It should (1) be related to the subject being taught and (2) be interesting enough to draw attention.

Cruising

Cruising around the classroom lets students know you might be close to them at any time. Walk around the room in different patterns; teach from the back and sides; walk to the middle. Cruising discourages disruptions, but if any occur, you can usually stop them quickly by moving close to correct the student involved. If the class won't quiet down, don't resort to yelling or manipulating with comments like "I love the way Paul is sitting. If everyone sits like Paul, we can line up for lunch!"

Cruising around the classroom, looking at every student, allows you to speak quietly (privacy), look directly at students (eye contact), and get close enough so they feel your presence (proximity) without making a scene. It allows you to unemotionally say, for example, "Please stop talking and get ready to learn," holding eye contact long enough for a student to feel you are talking directly to her, and then move to the next student. This method may sound time-consuming, but it rarely takes more than a minute or two because most students get the message after seeing your interaction with the first few students.

Perseverance

A common problem when we want students to stop doing something is lack of perseverance. A teacher asks a student to put away a cell phone or quiet down and then walks away. The student doesn't comply, so the teacher asks again, each time raising her voice until the student finally gets the message. The student ignored the first request because the teacher walked away, which—rightly or wrongly—shows a lack of commitment. We recommend a different approach. Walk over to the student and say, "Please put your cell phone away." Then, instead of walking away, stand right next to the student, resume teaching, and stay in the same place until the phone is put away. If nothing happens in a minute or two, give a gentle reminder but don't move. The student will get the message that you are serious and will most likely respond. For the few who don't, you can do one of two things: if the student is not distracting you or other students, ignore the behavior and deal with the student later; if the student is distracting, ask, "Do you want to put your phone away, or do you want me to hold on to it until after class?" In either case, persevere.

Lower Shields and Start Fresh

The Starship *Enterprise* was the name of the spaceship on the original *Star Trek* television series and movies. One of its defensive weapons was a shield, an energy force that surrounded the ship and protected it from attack. Using the shield, however, created problems. Communication outside the starship was impossible, and the shield drew energy from life-support systems. Students, too, have shields for the same defensive purpose, resulting in the same kinds of problems. When their shields are up, students are defensive, seeking protection from real or perceived psychological harm. Scowling and with arms folded, they send a clear message: "Leave me alone. I'm not happy. As long as these shields are raised, nothing positive will happen."

You may or may not know why students are so upset. It might be over an incident that happened yesterday. It might have nothing to do with you. Older students usually hold grudges for longer periods than younger students.

Regardless of whether or not you know about the precipitating incident, lowering shields requires the same resolving principle: start fresh. Whatever the cause of the upset, students need to know it's over. Try the following approaches.

- **Ask for an explanation.** "I can see you're not happy. I'd love to hear why, if you're willing to talk."
- **Try a diversion.** "I think you are still upset about what happened yesterday. Today is a new day and I'd like a fresh start. Did you see the ballgame [play any video games, catch anything interesting on Facebook, etc.] last night?"

- **Wait until the shield is lowered and things seem OK.**
Then try the following: "Sometimes you show me that you are very upset. When you feel that way, what do you want me to do to help?"
- **If the student shows no sign of lowering his shield, defer the intervention.** "I can see you aren't ready yet. I understand. I'm going to start fresh. I hope you join me soon. A good day is so much better than a bad one."

The Terminator

Another movie provides us with a very effective intervention that we call "The Terminator," after Arnold Schwarzenegger's first great *Terminator* movie. The Terminator had a tagline, "I'll be back," that forms the basis for this intervention. Use it when students refuse to engage when you are explaining a problem to them or just trying to have a conversation about behavior. They might reject you by covering their ears or asking you to leave them alone. They might passively reject by refusing to listen or turning away. When students behave this way, teachers tend to get angry and try to force them to listen. Unfortunately, we cannot force people to listen if they don't want to, and worse, even if we do get them to listen, we never get them to actually *hear* what we say. For this intervention to be effective, keep anger and frustration in check. Speak with a welcoming voice. Say, "I can see you won't talk with me right now. You may change your mind later, so I'll come back and try again." Then slowly and calmly walk away. Wait an appropriate amount of time (this will vary by age and individual personality; teenagers usually require longer wait time than young students) and return to say, "Is this a better time for us to talk?" If the student indicates it is not, then say, "You still don't want to talk. I understand. But you might change your mind in a while, so I'll be back and try again." Repeat as needed.

Be aware of students who indicate a willingness to listen but are really just trying to end the situation so you will "go away." They might say, "OK, let's get this over with," or "All right, what do you want?" Whatever you say next is likely a waste of breath. Very little will come of it except that the student will stop being "bothered."

We recommend saying, "I am glad you are ready to talk, but it seems that you are more ready to just get this over with. I want to listen and really hear what you think. Maybe I should try again later?" Be careful not to nag. Instead, wait and discuss the problem later. The message throughout this exchange should be "I won't give up on you because I care about you," not "Listen to me or I will wear you down until you do." The more you indicate that you are willing to listen as well as talk, the greater the chance for success.

Reframing

Teachers often tell us they are too angry and frustrated to stay calm during difficult situations. "It sounds easy to 'walk over' and say, in a calm voice, 'I can see you need more time to think.' But I struggle. I feel like saying, 'Shut up, you little bug. Who do you think you are?'" Keep practicing. We promise it gets easier.

A more constructive and applicable intervention is called "reframing" (Molnar & Linquist, 1990). The concept is quite simple. Reframing simply means "change the name of what you see." Changing the name usually changes the meaning and interpretation of our situation and can strongly influence how we interact. As reframing evolves from a classroom intervention to a life-long way of seeing what is before you, your life will change, too. Imagine being cut off by a speeding car. Your entire outlook changes depending on whether you think the driver is drunk or you think the driver needs to get to the hospital. You will never know the real reason, but which "thought" makes your day better?

Along the same lines but back in the classroom setting, which of the following statements has the more powerful effect and makes you feel better about the related issue?

"One thing I love about you is that no matter how difficult things get, you never give up. You are persistent. Most students your age give up so quickly when faced with difficulty, but not you. Sometimes, though, it makes more sense to realize you need to try something different. Want to talk about some other ways that might work better?"

"You are so stubborn. Why don't you ever do what I want you to do?"

There is no real difference between *persistent* and *stubborn*. They represent the same quality. In the first example, a student won't give up—a quality to be admired. In the second example, a student is stubborn and refuses to do what we want—a negative characteristic. The facts are much the same in these examples, but sometimes perception is everything. Every educator has the choice every day to see things positively or negatively—and everywhere in between. Find at least one positive adjective for every negative behavior. Doing so motivates students to hear your suggestions. It keeps you mentally strong. Anger and frustration dwindle, and every moment turns into something teachable.

Here's a true example of reframing that might have saved a student's life:

Sally Blake was a 3rd grade teacher of severely emotionally challenged and learning-disabled students in Kansas City, Missouri. "Rachel" had been sexually and physically abused at a very young age. She had severe emotional and learning difficulties. She was living in her third foster-care home in two years. Despite the terrible abuse, Rachel trusted Sally. "You are the only person I trust, because I know you will never hurt me."

Shortly after this emotional exchange, Sally caught Rachel stealing some of her personal items. Sally was livid and considered calling the police. Instead, she reframed the situation, paying particular attention to Rachel's words. If Sally was the only person Rachel trusted, then she didn't trust her newest foster parents. Perhaps she stole the items to have a part of Sally at home, making her feel safe and loved. Have you ever looked at a loved one's picture or reread a letter when that person was away? Rachel certainly lacked emotional and social skills to ask Sally for something personal. Sally decided that instead of a "thief," Rachel was really just "frightened, needy, and hurting." Sally gave Rachel one of her fancy belts and said, "Wear this belt whenever you need me, and imagine I am giving you a huge hug!" Obviously, giving a present to a student who steals is not the norm. Rachel was not like most students.

A year later, Rachel was institutionalized. The staff told Sally the belt might have saved Rachel's life. Rachel clutched it during a period of severe depression and repeated "Miss Blake loves me" over and over."[1] Without the belt, the staff believed, she might not have pulled through.

Reframing is not making an excuse. The goal is to find a solution that is otherwise unavailable. Reframing is easier when we remember that every choice has positive and negative results. The benefits must outweigh the costs for choices to work. This principle applies to student behavior as well. The student decided that, for whatever reason, the outcome that made us angry was worth the action. We can begin reframing by trying to understand the benefit of the choice as viewed by the student. This enables us to start the conversation with something positive before discussing the negative. The difference is more than semantic. It works when we are willing to accept a positive possibility for questionable behavior. We might not know what positive outcomes students are seeking, but by starting with a positive observation—even if it is wrong—we open the door for further discussion.

Keep in mind that an intervention or consequence can follow after reframing. Here are some examples:

1. A student hits another student after being called a name.

Teacher: I'm glad you defended yourself. No one has the right to hurt your feelings. Next time, though, try expressing with words instead of hands. Let's practice.

2. A student comes late for class.

Teacher: It's good to spend time with friends. They are important. School is equally important. Being on time matters. Thanks for listening.

3. A student doesn't do homework.

Teacher: It's good to be busy after school, and we all have difficult choices for how to spend our time. Is there a way to bump homework up on the priority list?

---

[1]Institutions for those with mental health issues do not allow patients to have belts, string, shoelaces, or anything else that can be used for inflicting self-harm. In Rachel's case, they made an exception because of her strong need to wear the belt, after a careful assessment that found her not to be at risk for suicide.

All situations can be reframed. Some require more effort than simply seeing things differently. Very strong interventions might be necessary if students are involved with gangs, drugs, or illegal activity. Even so, if you begin to address the concern with something positive, the chance for success is much better. For example, "I know you think of your gang as your brothers. Everyone needs to feel that kind of trust and protection. It makes us strong when we feel bad, especially about ourselves. Yet sometimes we have to say no, even to our brothers. Saying no requires more courage than anything else we might do. I hope you find a way to be that strong."

Managing Passive-Aggressive Behavior

People use passive-aggressive behavior when they believe they have lost power, or when they want to make a more powerful person suffer. People who use it are making three strong statements by their actions, and these statements cannot be ignored:

1. You are more powerful than me, but I still have enough power to punish you.

2. You can make me do what you want, but not the way you want it. I'll do it my way, and you won't like it.

3. This isn't over. You don't decide when it's over. I do.

As you can see by these statements, passive-aggressive behavior is used to regain power and control. It is an option for students who feel that their teachers are far more powerful and in control than they are.

Here are some examples of students' passive-aggressive behavior (notice the student complies in many of these examples, but not exactly as the teacher wants):

- Walking as slowly as possible when asked to do something
- Refusing to laugh when the teacher jokes about something
- Giving the teacher the silent treatment
- Playing the "Guess Why I'm Angry?" game
- Putting away their things, but taking a long time to do so
- Pouting or whining

Responding to Passive-Aggressive Behavior

The best way to stop passive-aggressive behavior is to avoid the traps of no-win situations. Say something such as this: "Right now I am going to ask you to move quicker, but because you don't like being told what to do, you are probably going to pretend not to hear me. Then I'll probably get annoyed, tell you to hurry up, and you will probably move even slower! So instead I am not going to say any of that. I will trust your decision to move faster."

Passive-aggressive individuals love to feel power by controlling other people's emotions. Do not allow this situation to develop. Sometimes passive-aggressive responses are triggered by unrecognized teacher slights or minor offenses from the past. The teacher may not even remember what happened, but the student continues to hold a grudge. Quite often, students might not tell or even know what triggered their passive-aggressive reaction. Most often a real or perceived lack of control over things affecting their lives is the core issue. Stay mentally tough and seek positive ways for these students to feel empowered and in control. Put them in positions of leadership (line leader, noise patrol, student representative, etc.). Ask their opinion.

Responding to passive-aggressive behavior is about teaching students to express wants and needs in a more productive way. When seeking solutions, look beyond the behavior to the likely cause, and privately begin a conversation by using any of the following openers:

- "I can see you are troubled by something that means a lot. Can we talk about it?"
- "I know you are not happy. Can I help you do something that will make things better?"
- "When I was your age, my teachers sometimes made me angry, but they didn't know what they did because I never told them. Teachers can sometimes be unaware of the things they do to their students. Is there something I did that's bothering you?"
- "When you slam the door like that, I know that you are trying to tell me in your own way how upset you are. Why don't we talk about what is really bothering you."

- "It is OK to feel angry when something upsets you. I appreciate you not hiding feelings from me. Please tell me directly when you're angry. You can say, 'I get angry when you . . . .' This is how we can figure things out."

The Two-Minute Intervention

The two-minute intervention is a strategy designed to combat passive-aggressive behavior, although it can be used as an intervention with other behavioral interruptions as well. It should be done privately, although you can use it during class when something other than direct instruction is happening—for example, during a group project or study-buddy review. This intervention is based on the belief that students would prefer not to be passive-aggressive with a teacher who they believe cares about them.

These are the steps for the two-minute intervention (if you cannot follow them exactly, do the best you can):

1. Spend two minutes talking conversationally with the target student for 10 consecutive days. Make the conversation informal. Do not talk about academics, performance, or behavior.

2. Talk about a topic of interest to the student. If you don't know the student's interests, use the time to find out. If the student is reluctant to share, talk about your interests and end your share with "How about you?" If you know nothing about the topic, ask the student to tell you about it; for example, "You and I like very different kinds of music. Can you tell me about why you like your favorite bands?"

3. At the beginning, be prepared to do most, if not all, of the talking. By the end of the 10 days, the ratio is usually reversed.

4. Be prepared for initial rejection, especially with older students. Because most have become accustomed to negative interactions, they are initially suspicious of adults who show interest. Don't be deterred. Remind yourself, if necessary, that it is only two minutes, and tomorrow is a new day. Things will most likely change if you keep at it.

5. Don't lie. Don't pretend to know, care about, or do anything that you don't.

6. Work with one student at a time. This activity requires emotional courage and energy.

Final Thoughts

The informal discipline system is about finding caring ways—without consequences—to resolve most classroom problems. Whereas consequences are formal responses to a specific rule violation, an informal intervention is a response to inappropriate behavior that is based primarily on how we interact with the student. Consider planning how you might use these informal methods right now. For example, think of a particularly challenging student in your class who seems to require constant reminders to behave appropriately. How might you reframe his behavior? Really try to picture this student as "determined" or "strong-willed" instead of "annoying" or "frustrating." Do you see how you might be able to find more opportunities for positive interaction with the student? Finally, consider initiating a "two-minute intervention" with this student. If you aren't currently teaching, try this exercise with a person who rubs you the wrong way.

8

Interrupting Misbehavior with Good Teaching

Motivated students rarely cause behavior problems. Enthusiastic teachers who present material in stimulating, meaningful ways and treat students with respect and dignity can make any subject come alive, and a teacher who doesn't motivate can make any subject die. The not-so-secret way to interrupt negative behavior is less about what we teach and more about how we teach it. The Pearson Foundation study (2014) cited in Chapter 5 found only 38 percent of middle and high school students feel that classes help them understand what is happening in their everyday lives. Forty-seven percent say school is boring, and only 31 percent feel that teachers make their class an exciting place for students to learn.

In this chapter we explore how to design and deliver lessons that motivate students, with examples of motivating classroom activities that any teacher can use. We also discuss three areas that often trigger behavior problems in school—evaluation and grading, homework, and independent group work—and present ideas for including motivating elements in each area as a way to minimize misbehavior.

Lessons That Motivate Students

There are hundreds of ways to design and deliver lessons that motivate students. We will examine four of the most powerful motivating elements, along with classroom activities that can be used in any content area and are designed to meet the basic needs of students. The four motivating elements are as follows:

- Relevance to students' lives
- Teacher passion for the subject matter
- Personal concern for each student
- Fun

Relevance to Students' Lives

Subject matter that connects to students' lives is a powerful way to prevent behavior problems. Relevance reduces misbehavior because all students will listen if what they are learning helps them get better at something they already love or understand something they experience in a new way. For example, although "fake news" has become an issue that many students hear about, 80 percent of middle school students can't tell the difference between a sponsored article and a real news story (Wineburg, 2013). A teacher we know had her students read the homepage of a website on Martin Luther King Jr. and asked them what the author was trying to say. The most common answer was "how great Martin Luther King Jr. was." She then asked students to read the other pages of the website, whereupon they discovered that it was a white supremacist diatribe on the evils of King supported with phony evidence. The stunned students learned how easily fake news can influence thought.

Although not every lesson can connect with students' lives, the more lessons that can, the better the instructional experience will be. We know that students are highly motivated to learn and talk about peer relationships. They have a strong need to belong. You can connect this need to many aspects of a curriculum. For example, any lesson that involves conflict can be connected to how powerful the need to belong is and how it can create natural competition for respect, resources, and dignity. Unfortunately, one way to fulfill these critical needs is to spew hate speech at other groups (which may or may not be an issue in your school or community). This point can lead to a discussion of the differences between teasing, sarcasm, insults, and hate speech. Students can explore questions such as these: Does the intention of the speaker matter? Is all hate speech the same? Does a victim of hate speech have the right to use it to fight back? Such discussions can set the stage for developing the formal discipline system or underpin the need for a classroom value that all cultures be respected, along with related rules and consequences. (See Curwin, 2017, for more on this topic.)

One of the best ways to create relevant lessons is to listen to your students. Let them know that you appreciate their time and their thoughts. Start by promising not to waste student time. You might say something such as this to your class:

> I want to let you all know that beginning right now, I will always do my best never to waste your time. I hate when people waste mine, and I will try hard not to waste yours. This means I will do my best to give you relevant work based on your skill set. I will not give you homework just so you are not playing video games or watching television at night. You might not like all the assignments I give, and you might not understand why I give them; but remember, I promise to do my best never to waste your time. If you feel like I am wasting your time, please see me privately so we can discuss what's going on and maybe find a better alternative. Now I want you to tell me what you need to get the most out of this class and to learn as much as you possibly can.

Teacher Passion for the Subject Matter

As we said earlier, passion is essential to great teaching and probably makes learning much more interesting. If you think of your favorite movie stars, musicians, and athletes—the ones you will pay to watch—all perform with passion. One way to teach with passion is to always include one aspect of the lesson, content, activity, or story that you personally love. Think about doing that as you walk in the classroom door. Many of your most difficult students see only negative passion at home in the form of fighting or hurting others. Experiencing passion in learning is a healthy alternative.

You can also do an activity that gives students an opportunity to identify the teacher characteristics they most value. Doing so may give you some ideas of what aspects of yourself to emphasize so you can best connect with them. Divide the class into groups of three to five students; give each group a large sheet of poster paper and a handful of crayons. Ask them to draw an abstract picture of what they believe is a great teacher, using no words. Everything students include in the drawing must be approved unanimously. After the pictures are finished, create an art gallery by taping them on the wall, and give each group a chance to explain what their picture means. You are likely to discover a number of things you can do or are already doing to motivate your class.

Personal Concern for Each Student

When troubled students are asked why they listen to some teachers and not others, the most common answers include "They care about me" and "They believe in me." Teachers who are successful in conveying these messages design lessons that show an understanding of their students' basic needs. As we know, the school years are key to the formation of *identity*. Most students love to think and learn about themselves. You can tap this need in order to help them build emotional strength and an understanding of how feelings influence choices.

There are hundreds of classroom activities that focus on learning about oneself. Few behavior distractions occur during such activities because we all like to talk and learn about ourselves. Here are 10 activities that you can build lessons around or connect to the curriculum.

1.   Have your students create a "book of me." The content may include pictures or self-portraits of the student; pictures or drawings of things the student loves; things the student is good at, places the student has visited, and pictures of family and pets. Decide in advance whether these books will be shared with other students, so everyone can decide how much personal information to include. It is more fun to share books, but the prospect of sharing may lead some students to reveal less about themselves that is important and meaningful.

2.   Have students write a story about something that wasn't funny when it happened but is funny now.

3.   Have students write essays about something they want to do that is exciting, dangerous, or scary, like sky diving, scuba

diving, racing on a track, or mountain climbing. The paper must include research that includes scientific facts about the activity, its history, and why they want to try it.

4.   Create a "unique board." The goal of this activity is to show students both what they have in common and how they are different. Make two bulletin boards—one titled "Me Too," the other, "Only Me." Working on their own, students try to think of something they are good at, a special place they have visited, or something they really like. They post these on the "Only Me" side of the board. If anyone else in the room has experienced or likes the same thing, that student adds his name on the note and moves it to the "Me Too" side. The goal is for as many students as possible to have an item remain on the "Only Me" side.

5.   Have students make a list of five activities they love to do and have already done at least once. Then they must find a partner who shares at least three activities on their list. Once paired, they share why they like the activity. Invariably, some students will not find a partner. Pair those students up and have them share what is on their lists.

6.   Choose a book the class is reading and ask each student to imagine he is the main character. Each student then must tell the class about something the character has done that he would change. This can also be done with historical figures in a social studies class.

7.   Ask your students to think about five places they love to go and five places they must go to that they hate (such as the dentist's office). Then ask them to make a list of five people they really like and five they don't (note that they may not include classmates on their "dislike" lists). Ask them to imagine going to the place they like with one person they dislike. Then reverse the proposal. Ask them to imagine going to a place they hate with someone they like. Which of the two experiences do they like better? Why? How can they use this activity to improve what they do?

8.   Have students write a paper on something that they were afraid of when they were younger but that no longer frightens them. What changed this fearful thing to something harmless?

9.   Role-play in class a situation in which you are telling a student to do something and the student doesn't want to do it. Before the student responds, ask the students who are watching to brainstorm a list of best student responses. Finish the role-play by trying some of the suggestions. If a student defies you after this role-play, compare that student's response to the best responses in the student-created list.

10. Do the same role-play activity, but change roles. In this case, the student asks the teacher for something the teacher doesn't want to do. Follow the same steps as before.

Fun

Disruption can often be interrupted with a fun activity. For example, you can challenge your students to solve a riddle:

The more you have of it, the less you see. What is it?

The more you take from me, the bigger I get. What am I?

The answers are given somewhere in this chapter. Are you curious to know? Are you more or less likely to keep reading? If this was a lesson we were teaching, we could put these riddles on the board and tell students that the answers are hidden somewhere in the lesson and then challenge them to be on the lookout. With a student who struggles academically, occasionally give the answer in advance so he looks good in front of his peers. (By the way, the answer to the first riddle is "darkness"; the answer to the second is "hole.")

A worthy goal of every lesson is to surround learning with as much joy as possible. One of the best ways to create joyful lessons is to make a list of the kinds of activities you intend to use in your classroom and then ask for student feedback. Try to be specific as possible. You may need to show or explain some of the activities. Here are some examples:

- Listen to a lecture
- Engage in classroom discussion
- Read a story
- Solve a riddle

- Try an experiment
- Find the answer to a hard question (in a group)
- Write a song about the lesson (in a group)
- Make an advertisement about a lesson (in a group)
- Write and perform a play about a topic
- Read out loud
- Read silently
- Make a poster about the lesson (in a group)

Hand out your list of activities and ask students to rate each on a scale of 1 (least fun) to 5 (most fun). Collect and review the lists, paying particular attention to those that come from students most likely to disrupt. Include as many of their highly rated activities as you possibly can.

Even difficult units can incorporate an element of fun. Here is an example of how you might combine content and fun to prepare students for such a unit—in this case, a new unit on fractions: Divide your class into groups of three or four students and explain how advertisements work. Most of them probably already know that the purpose of ads is to get people to think that if they buy something, their life will be better in some way. Then assign each group to perform a skit, write and sing a jingle, and make a poster advertising at least a few important benefits of knowing about fractions. With this activity, your students are not only tapping their creativity and having fun, but also relating positively to the subject before it is even taught.

Evaluation and Grading That Motivate Students

After his team lost in the NBA finals, LeBron James, arguably the best player to ever play basketball, said, "I put in the work. . . . Does it always result in winning? . . . No. . . . Like I've always told myself, if you feel like you put in the work and you leave it out on the floor, then you can always push forward and not look backwards" (Zillgitt, 2017).

We have discussed the power of effort throughout this book. Perhaps its most important application is in the evaluation of learning. The issue of which is of higher value, effort or achievement, has been and will forever be debated. We believe that in an instructional environment, effort is always more important. No student can do more than try. The highest achievement is always the result of the best effort. We have said over the years that a student would rather be bad than stupid. Students have no control over their achievement, but they can control how much effort they put forth to achieve.

It has long been known that it is not success that matters, but the reason for the success (Weiner, 1972). Easy work offers no pride. Natural ability is great for those who have it, but if students with different abilities are compared to each other, the only winners are those with a particular skill. The only attribute that is controlled by students across the board in a positive way is effort. In addition, the best way to keep students motivated when they don't achieve a goal is to redefine "failure" as "not yet." One of the authors is a terrible speller but felt better when told, "You are a good speller. You just haven't learned all the words yet."

Steve Wozniak, the inventor of the Apple computer, believes that failure is an abstract concept that has no real meaning. When asked by one of the authors how he dealt with failure, he answered, "I don't know. It's never happened yet. If it does, I'll let you know." With a somewhat different viewpoint in mind, schools would do well to borrow from billion-dollar companies such as Google and Intuit that hold "failure parties." According to Intuit cofounder Scott Cook, "We celebrate failure because every failure teaches something important that can be the seed for the next great idea" (Alge, 2015).

Talk to your students about mistakes. Explain that failure is on the path to success and that success rarely happens without mistakes. Remind them that they all probably fell several times while learning to walk. Ask them to identify other skills they have now that were once in the "not yet" category. If students understand this idea, they become more willing to try. You might ask your students to keep track of all the mistakes they make for a day or week and what they learned from each. Consider popping some balloons at the end of the interval in celebration.

To motivate difficult students or to interrupt their pattern of negative behavior, give them a realistic chance of achieving the best grade possible if they put forth their best effort. One way to know if they are putting forth effort is to compare their current work and behavior with their previous work and behavior. By contrast, competitive grading can destroy motivation and invite discipline problems: "Kristie's paper is an *A*, which means Freddie's paper must be a *C* because it is not as good as Kristie's." If this mind-set prevails in the classroom, Freddie learns he has no chance of ever getting an *A* because he isn't as good as Kristie and probably never will be.

When people in any profession learn that their best is not good enough, they have limited options. One is to quit. When a singer can't hit certain notes any longer, she often retires. On the other hand, students can't walk away from, say, 2nd grade. They stay and often disrupt. Then when they fail, they think, "Yeah, but I didn't even try." Another option is to cheat. Some sports players choose this option. Their best is not good enough, so they take performance-enhancing drugs. Some students will choose to cheat. They think, "I need a 90 average to make honor roll. I know I can't get a 90 myself, so let me copy someone who can." One could argue that at least cheaters care. A technique to combat these two choices is to challenge students to compete with themselves. Here is an example of a teacher who did this and saw tremendous success.

Mr. Lester taught an 8th grade class of tough students. The previous year, these students had rarely received grades higher than a *C*, and most averages were closer to *D+*. Mr. Lester decided to give all the students an *A* on their first assignment no matter what their work on that assignment looked like. Without telling them, *he also decided that of the first five grades of the quarter, none would be lower than a B*. Mr. Lester's goal was to see if higher grades made students feel as if they had something to lose. Many disruptive, unmotivated, and unproductive students have been taught to hold tight to what they have—which is why most won't take off their headphones, hats, and jackets; no one buys them a new one if it gets stolen or lost. Mr. Lester took the same approach with grades. He also had nothing to lose. "They were already doing poorly, so why not try something different?" he told us.

Mr. Lester began the second quarter by telling the students that they could all maintain their *A*s or *B*s by improving individual performance. This message was repeated the two next quarters, but the work Mr. Lester required increased each time. Most students tried hard to keep their good grades, a prize they had never known before.

Once students believe a good grade is achievable through effort, they put forth more energy to maintain it even if doing so means more work. A system of evaluation that forces students to compete with each other or that uses the same criteria for all students, despite intellectual and academic differences, produces winners and losers. The losers often become discipline problems. They have learned that hard work and best effort are not rewarded. Few of us can do our best for very long with such minimal validation. What Mr. Lester did with his class is impossible if we care more about *grades* than we do about *learning*.

A key to having evaluation contribute to hope and belief in success is to involve students in the process. Here are some ways to do that:

- Ask students to help write test questions.
- Allow students to choose how many questions a test or quiz should have.
- Incorporate student ideas as to what information should be on the test.
- Have students test each other (this is usually done more for practice). Because of the importance of privacy, students should not see the grade of another student.
- Allow students to replace a few test questions with others on the same subject that they feel more confident about answering.
- Include the three Rs—redo, retake, and revise—for tests and homework. To keep things manageable, set time limits (e.g., "You have three days to improve your essay"). Be sure to tell students you will determine their new grade after the makeup work is complete.
- Occasionally allow students to grade themselves, especially on assignments requiring creativity and without a right or wrong answer. Base the criteria on a rubric or outline you've presented before the assignment.

However you personally choose to define or incorporate "failure," remember that the goal of school is for students to learn. It doesn't matter what they can't do, only what they can. For troubled students, their lives may depend on this distinction.

Motivating Students to Do Homework

One of the most persistent battles between students and teachers revolves around homework. Can you even calculate the amount of time you spend dealing with discipline related to homework? Two possibilities for addressing the homework issue are (1) allowing students to choose which days homework will be assigned and (2) making homework optional. Let's take a closer look at each of these.

Giving Students a Choice

Elsewhere in this book we have discussed the importance of student choice as a way to minimize disruptions, and the idea can apply to homework by allowing students to choose which nights they would prefer to have homework assigned. You might introduce the idea by saying something like this:

> Class, I will be giving homework two or three nights per week this year. Many teachers think they are being nice by giving homework Monday through Thursday and none on Fridays. I might do that, but I want to give you a choice. I realize many of you are tired after school. Some of you have practice or some type of music event. I know many of your parents work during the week and are tired themselves at night. If you have a parent who travels or works late, they might not be home to help. So you decide. Would you prefer three nights Monday through Thursday, or one night Monday through Thursday and a bit more on Fridays?

Let's say the students select Tuesday and Friday. That decision helps structure the lives of parents. At parent night, you might say something like this:

> Parents, I just want to let you know how my class works this year. I promise to do my best not to waste your or your child's time. This means I won't give homework every night. It will normally be

on Tuesdays and Fridays. Please set aside at least one hour every Tuesday night to work with your son or daughter, if possible. If they come home on Tuesdays and say they don't have homework, ask again! If you want to put them in a sports league or have them take music lessons, please do it on a night other than Tuesday, if possible.

Most parents will be happy with this approach because it reduces the amount of nagging they may have to do with their son or daughter about homework. Some will ask why you are assigning homework on Fridays. You can simply say, "The class voted and picked Tuesdays and Fridays."

This approach also gives the teacher more leverage when the homework is not done. Let's say a student comes unprepared on Monday morning. It is now much easier to imagine the following exchange:

Teacher: Why isn't the homework done? I'm disappointed that you did not follow through on your decision to have homework on Fridays. I guess from now on I will decide which nights you get homework.

Student: No, we can make decisions.

Teacher: Good. You have another chance. From now on I do not want to hear any stories about why the work isn't done.

Homework is a topic that leads to many power struggles and unmotivated students. Consider the following example:

Teacher: Do problems 1 through 10.

Student: I do not want to do 10 problems.

An argument ensues. But if the teacher focuses more on the outcome of the homework and not so much on the number of problems, the situation becomes much easier to handle:

Teacher: Do problems 1 through 10.

Student: I do not want to do 10 problems.

Teacher: OK, that's fine. How many do you want to do?

Student: None.

Teacher: None is not an option. I'd have no idea if you learned what I taught. I can live with 5. In fact, you decide which 5 will best show me you understand the material, and do those.

Making Homework Optional

Educators who want to completely eliminate the hassle of homework can make homework optional. Top students may not need the practice that is part of many homework assignments, and students who choose not to do homework but perform adequately on tests or other measures of learning will still be able to pass the class. Students who don't do homework and fail on measures of evaluation may be able to more clearly see the connection between the practice they need but aren't doing and the results they're getting. Making that connection might provide the motivation they need. In all cases, it becomes unnecessary to have power struggles over the homework issue. A better option is for students who do the homework to bank extra points toward their grade; so instead of facing negative consequences for not doing homework, students can earn a bonus that can be applied if needed.

Students will do homework more often when it

- Allows students to work collaboratively with others.
- Requires multiple skills and intelligences.
- Has observable value to the students.
- Has an appropriate level of challenge (is not seen as busywork).
- Is returned quickly by the teacher.
- Allows for student choice.
- Is appropriate for the students' age and abilities.
- Is for review, practice, or application rather than teaching something new.

Homework and the "Flipped Classroom"

Perhaps the most significant instructional innovation we have seen since the last edition of this book was published—one that changes the concept of homework and has the potential to dramatically affect behavior management—is the "flipped classroom." This concept offers a way to differentiate instruction but requires no more preparation than usual for an academically diverse group of students, including those with special needs. Students can learn at their own rate and level without the teacher needing to prepare numerous lessons or variations of the same lesson.

In the flipped classroom, the teacher makes a video recording of each lesson instead of presenting it in class, and students are assigned to watch it for homework. Students learn the lesson as well as they can by watching the recording, formulate any questions they may have for greater understanding, and bring those questions to class. The classroom teacher can instruct students to watch and listen for particular points that are especially important. Class time that in a traditional classroom is devoted to direct instruction is instead spent practicing or applying skills, answering questions, working on group projects, or working on papers and other assignments that are traditionally done at home. The teacher moves among the students to help, guide, challenge, and work with individuals or small groups. She may occasionally use direct group instruction or whole-class discussion to clarify or reinforce the material, especially when several students are struggling with the same concept; but most classroom time is used to help struggling students, provide enrichment for advanced students, and oversee the progress of all students.

Within this structure, students who have quickly mastered the material can move on and watch the next lesson on their tablet or laptop. Students whose minds wander can simply rewind and have the information repeated as many times as they'd like. Students who are far behind can work on material suited to their skill level and move along at their pace. If a special education teacher or aide is present, students can get the help they need without calling attention to themselves because a single lesson is rarely if ever being taught to the whole class. Students who didn't watch the lesson can use their class time to watch. The beauty of a well-structured flipped classroom is that everyone has something to do at the appropriate level and is working at an appropriate pace all the time—which is a recipe for more success and fewer behavior problems.

Either the teacher assigned to a certain class or another who teaches the same subject or grade level records each lesson. If more than one teacher is teaching the same subject or grade level, they can alternate. Because lessons are stored digitally, they can be used until there are changes to the curriculum. Ideally, teachers from different schools who are teaching from the same curriculum can share their lessons so that students with a preference for one or another teacher's style can choose their preferred teacher's recorded lesson without having to switch classes. The classroom teacher remains vital to the learning process, but personality and style become less of a factor because students don't have to rely on direct instruction to learn. Although the basics of how to set up a flipped classroom have been specified (Bergmann & Sams, 2012), educators can adapt the model in many ways to fit their subject and style.

Making Independent Group Work More Effective

With challenging students, independent group work is usually either a hit or a bust, depending upon how it is structured. Here is a step-by-step guide to making group work effective.

1. **Take charge of putting students in groups.** Given a choice, students tend to work with the same classmates. There are many other situations that allow for students to choose. This isn't one of them.

2. **Announce "No complaints allowed."** Before group work begins, you can say, "Please do not complain about who you are working with. I will mix up the partners often this year."

3. **Limit groups to five students.** We prefer to have six groups of five instead of five groups of six. Odd numbers work better than even ones, and the group is less likely to self-divide into smaller discussions.

4. **After students are in groups, tell them the "two Ts":** **time and task.** You can say, "You have eight minutes to get this done. How many minutes?" Ask students to repeat how much time they get, and then assign them the task. For groups that finish

before the others, have in mind something for them to do that is constructive and related to the lesson.

Remember that it is easier to extend than to take away. It is better to provide less time than you think an activity is going to require. If you think the task should take 10 minutes, tell the class they have 5. Giving less time creates urgency. If students finish quickly, bring the group back into the whole-class structure. If students are not finished after 5 minutes, you can extend time. Take time away and be ready to hear, "You said we had 10 minutes and it's only been 7!"

5. After telling the "two Ts," number each student one through five. Each number corresponds with a specific job for that assignment.

6. Make sure your number ones are group leaders. Group leaders hold the most important role in the group. Their job requires ensuring that everyone else does their job at a high level. Leaders also help students who struggle with their roles. Disruptive students are often excellent group leaders.

7. Assign all other roles. Number two is the reader. Number three takes notes. Number four organizes notes so number five can present to the class. All students must work together to complete the task.

8. Ask group members to follow their leaders. You can say, "During groups you are allowed to talk to the teacher if you are a group leader. If there is a problem with your role or you are unclear about directions, please go to your group leader first. If they can't help, they come to me." Instead of worrying about 30 students, the teacher now has to worry about 6 leaders.

9. Give each group leader red, yellow, and green cups to signal progress. Red means "stop" (our group is stuck and needs lots of help); yellow means "slow down" (we have a quick question like "How do we pronounce this word?"); green means the group needs no help. The teacher watches the room and communicates only with group leaders.

Remember that students are easily distracted when you repeatedly ask if things are OK in the group. Like a diner's nod to a waiter, the colored-cup technique lets you know when you are needed. Of course, you can touch base occasionally with each group to be sure it is functioning properly.

10. Think carefully before switching group roles. It is best during group time to put people in roles that fit them best. The Golden State Warriors do not move Steph Curry from guard to center just to change it up. One exception is the role of number five—the speaker/presenter—because presenting ideas in a public forum or a job interview is an important life skill rarely taught in school. Think of group work as a business. The teacher is the CEO. The CEO's name is on the door. But any good business also has a director of sales and marketing, a director of human resources, and a director of public relations. There needs to be a special reason for a regular salesperson to go directly to the CEO. The CEO usually says, "Ask your manager first before you come to me."

At first these steps may seem like they require a lot of work to implement. But following them creates a structure that enables students to quickly learn how to gain maximum benefit from working in groups.

9

Managing Stress Effectively

Despite the overwhelmingly positive reaction to *Discipline with Dignity* when it was first published, some educators claimed the content was too "humanistic." Particularly targeted for criticism were the 13 pages of "strategies for reducing stress" that contained meditative breathing exercises and guided visualizations, among other techniques (Curwin & Mendler, 1988). Although the exercises were designed to calm the mind and had no religious basis, apparently critics saw no place for them in school. Although these strategies were presented as ways for educators to stay calm, we also suggested that most students, including those with behavior problems and students with difficulties paying attention, could benefit. At that time, it was rare for any school to offer these practices to teachers through professional development or to students during the school day. They were negatively labeled as "touchy-feely." Nowadays, these kinds of strategies, while still not entirely mainstream in schools, are offered as viable practices to both teachers and students. In fact, some schools teach difficult students "mindfulness" practices as an alternative to detention (Haupt, 2016). Teachers need only go online or pick up a book to learn about many such strategies (David, 2009; Jennings & Siegel, 2015; Mendler, 2014; Shirley & MacDonald, 2016). We applaud such practices and encourage their expansion.

Teacher stress is higher than at any time we can remember. Gallup (2014) found that 46 percent of teachers reported high daily levels of stress during the school year—a percentage that tied for the highest rate among all occupational groups! High-stakes testing, pressure to finish the curriculum, lack of decision-making autonomy, inflexible scripted teaching programs that leave no room for creative innovation, highly structured and labor-intensive behavior programs, along with many other factors, all contribute.

Job-related stress can be handled in two basic ways: change the external causes of it, or change our internal response to it. This chapter focuses on the latter. Because teacher state of mind and accompanying behavior are among the most important influences on our students, it is important that we manage feelings of stress so we do not start counting the days until vacation on the first day of school. For this reason, we broaden the discussion of stress in this chapter to include some important factors in addition to the challenges posed by disruptive students. When students cooperate, we feel good about them and ourselves. Identifying and meeting the basic needs of our students is the single best way to reduce their stress and ours.

Stress and Discipline

In virtually all surveys, educators identify student behavior as a major stressor (Greenburg, Brown, & Abenavoli, 2016). According to Antoniou, Polychroni, and Vlachakis (2006), the greatest sources of stress for teachers are problems related to interacting with students, addressing lack of student interest in school, and handling students with "difficult" behaviors—in essence, problems with motivation and discipline. If we internalize stress, the consequences may include headaches, exhaustion, sleeplessness, pain, and feelings of inadequacy. If we externalize stress, we start disliking the child and everyone else responsible for aiding or supporting the inappropriate behavior. Unhealthy teacher responses to stress often fall into one of four categories: the Conflict Avoider, the Muscle Flexer, the Marine Sergeant, and the Guilt Giver. Let's look at each of these in turn.

The Conflict Avoider

Teachers who are Conflict Avoiders are often willing to ignore misbehavior because they fear conflict. They apologetically set limits and rarely follow through with consequences when rules are broken. Such teachers prefer to give themselves headaches, back pain, and other forms of physical tension rather than feel guilty for acting "mean" to their students. They are often overly nice and may try to act "cool," hoping for the kind of acceptance friends seek. Disruptive students see these teachers as weak and ineffective and take control of the classroom because teachers are at their mercy. These teachers are usually high up on the "wish list" of difficult students because they can have their way in their classes. It is not unusual to have widespread chaos without the teacher noticing or responding. Children show little respect because they respect teachers who are firm, are fair, set limits, and treat them with dignity and respect.

The Muscle Flexer

Muscle Flexers adopt the attitude "I do not care if they like me or not, but they better do what I want—or else." They often resort to power-based methods of getting their way, including open confrontation. They invite resistance, retaliation, and rebellion. Muscle Flexers shout from across the room and make examples of students, hoping others will be deterred. These teachers are quick to write referrals and send students to the office but often complain that administration is too soft. Unless these teachers have a warm and caring support system outside school, they are likely to receive so few positive strokes on the job that they experience loss of enthusiasm and early burnout. They usually cynically express dissatisfaction to anyone who will listen and rarely reveal anything personal to students for fear of becoming vulnerable. Apologizing is not an option because blame usually belongs elsewhere. Most children *dislike* this type of teacher, and most Muscle Flexers don't really care. They do not usually have to deal with a lot of persistent behavior problems because they are often successful at getting difficult children removed from their classrooms.

The Marine Sergeant

The Marine Sergeant is the Muscle Flexer's first cousin. The Marine Sergeant's attitude is "Everybody gets treated the same way in here, and there are no exceptions to the rule." This approach is justified with their definition of the word *fairness*. Because of how rigid this approach is, pride gets in the way of what is best for students. Tough-to-reach students see rigidity as an invitation to disrupt. Although their tight structure can be an asset to students whose lives lack consistency, Marine Sergeants are usually unable to reach difficult students who need flexibility. Differentiation is not usually in their vocabulary. These teachers follow policy or procedure to the letter, even when the results are continually ineffective.

The Guilt Giver

Guilt Givers often say, "Can't you see how miserable I feel when you misbehave? Pleeeaaase stop" or "Look at all I do for you, and you are so ungrateful!" They excuse inappropriate behavior with the expectation that students will feel grateful and return the favor with cooperation and affection. When that doesn't happen, they complain, hoping students will come to their senses. Such teachers feel personally hurt and angry when students misbehave because they expect students to appreciate and reciprocate their goodwill. When guilt doesn't work, they become angry. Some internalize the resentment and emotionally withdraw or become passive-aggressive. Others externalize with direct expressions of hostility toward the nonresponsive student that quickly lead to conflict escalation. Guilt Givers are likely to have numerous interpersonal difficulties because of blocked feelings, which lead to high levels of stress and burnout.

Strategies for Reducing Stress

Given the major consequences that stress has for teachers—and their students—it is important to find ways to reduce it. Here we offer several strategies for doing just that.

Anticipate the Predictable

In many ways, teaching is highly predictable. We know the exact days of the week we will work, the exact hours we will be at school, and the exact location we are going to be in. We know that our "customers" come every day, whether we are good at our job or not. We can even closely estimate how much money we will make during our working lifetime, from the first day of our first year on the job! Yet when it comes to behavior, even veteran teachers seem taken aback.

A major key in effectively handling stress is to stop being surprised at what students say and do. For example, think about what often happens when a teacher corrects a student and then attempts to walk away. The student mumbles something barely loud enough to hear but not loud enough to make a scene. Unfortunately, many teachers hear the mumbling and get trapped by their stress. Trying to protect their authority, they stop, turn around, and provocatively ask, "What did you say to me?" Every student replies one of two ways: the not-so-difficult students say, "Nothing"; the tough students say something like "I called you an asshole." Either way, tension increases.

Anticipating the predictable can greatly reduce stress. Nothing good comes from asking a student, "What did you say?" (Do you really want to know the answer?) Stop confronting difficult students with this question! Do not get hooked. Continue walking away and do not go back. Let the student have the last word for now. Let students know that you will not always stop class to handle misbehavior. Explain that if it looks like you are ignoring the behavior, it is only because you consider what you are teaching to be more important in that moment than reacting to the behavior, and you will decide what to do with the misbehaving students later.

We recently consulted in an elementary school near Hilton Head, South Carolina. Before asking us to work with four teachers who were struggling with discipline, the principal wanted us to watch the teacher she considered to be the best in the school. Ms. Evans was about 5-feet-5-inches tall and 100 pounds, and she greeted us with the same cheerful "Good morning" that met each student. About midway through her math lesson, a young boy in the back threw a wadded-up piece of paper at a girl two desks away. Ms. Evans turned around just in time to see the release of the paper and the girl get hit. The entire class watched to see what she would do. Ms. Evans immediately instructed the students to "put their eyes back on their own papers." She then walked over to Tyquan, the boy who threw the paper. As privately as possible, in a firm yet nonaggressive tone, she said, "Throwing things at other people in this class is unacceptable. What can we do to make sure this does not happen again?" Tyquan looked back at Ms. Evans and said, "I hate this stupid class. It is so boring, and besides, I have no idea what I'm doing, anyway." Ms. Evans replied, "After class we will talk about this privately, and I promise to make things better for you in here. But for now, what do you think you should say to Yolanda [the girl hit by the paper]?" Ms. Evans defused the student, kept him in class, got everyone else on track, and even convinced Tyquan to apologize without telling him to do so.

Ms. Evans told us she rarely gets stressed because "He's 8. That's what some 8-year-olds do. No 8-year-old makes me mad unless I allow it." Some children swear, others are rude, a few are forgetful, some won't be able to sit still, and others struggle to understand the material. Knowing what students are going to do before they do it helped Ms. Evans easily defuse a potentially volatile situation.

Some children are good at triggering stress, but only because they know exactly what to do and say to push our buttons. But because predictability works both ways, we have to be a step ahead of them. If we are ready for students who are late, unprepared, and rude, we don't have to allow their behavior to get us riled. Instead of expressing annoyance and frustration, which is likely to reinforce a student's hostility, we can smile and say, "I'm smiling because I knew you were going to say that. If you want to get the reaction you're looking for, get to class on time, bring your books, and be polite. Then I'll be shocked—I promise!"

Develop Mental Toughness

The best way for us to manage stress is to choose our attitude! We can decide to *stay personally connected without taking personally what students may do and say.* People who are the best at their jobs in any profession usually stay calm under pressure. Their focus is on using and managing whatever resources they have the ability to control. Mental toughness means controlling our own "buttons." It means deciding what is worth getting hyped up about and what isn't. It means that when students get stressed, the teacher gets calmer. *Staying personally connected to children means...*

> I will not give up on you.
>
> I will not quit on you.
>
> I will not lose control with you.
>
> I will not yell at you unless I believe it is necessary for you to hear.
>
> I will reframe my feelings of anger.
>
> I will always be here no matter what.
>
> Because I am a teacher and my job is to show you a better way, *I will not take personally what you do or say when I do not like it.*

The best teachers are wise enough to know that objectionable behavior is not about them. Somewhere some students learned to talk in a disrespectful way. They learned to hit instead of use words. They were taught that the way they are behaving is actually the right way. When you feel your buttons starting to get pushed, before you react, try hearing or seeing what the student said or did in a neutral or even silly way. For example, imagine the student called you a "chair" rather than an "asshole." Your immediate reaction would likely be to feel concern for the student rather than anger at her disrespect.

Have a Healthy Perspective

Our obligation is to be at our best for all students all the time. But this is not usually realistic. No matter how hard we try, none of us are at the top of our game every minute. Like a great ballplayer who strikes out, great teachers make mistakes. Keep your head in the game and do not make the same mistake twice. Review the situation later to see what you might do differently to avoid a recurrence. If you can't shake the feeling of being irritable, let students know. We know a teacher who shows her students a pair of unmistakably "ugly shoes" (steel toes, orange shoestrings, etc.) and tells them if they see her wearing these, it means she has little patience and they need to be extra thoughtful.

Turn the page as quickly as possible to keep a bad day from continuing on the same track. Was one or more of your students behaving badly? Did you do or say something you regret? If so, apologize and encourage the student to fix the behavior.

If you're having a bad day, try to determine the cause. Is it something within or beyond your control? At the very least, focus more on gratitude than resentment. For example, "Teaching is tough and can be exasperating but . . .

"I have a good-paying job in a spotty economy."

"As tough as it is, I'm not in the hospital fighting for my life."

"I have an opportunity every day to affect how students think and feel about themselves."

Network with a Colleague

When you need a break, consider networking with a trusted colleague. A fellow teacher, a school counselor, a psychologist, or a social worker can be a huge help. Develop prearranged signals with this person that tell them what kind of support you are looking for. For example, if you are sending a student to the office with a yellow pass, it means "I need a break from the child for 10 minutes." A purple scarf means "I'm ready to lose it and need 20 minutes." Knowing you have a place to send a student creates peace of mind.

Become Predictably Unpredictable

Being unpredictable can take many forms: wear silly clothes, bring in guest speakers, take students on field trips, sing songs, play games (but without forcing competition), dance, or rap. Most important, enjoy yourself and have fun.

One of the authors remembers one lesson from 26 years ago in 9th grade Earth Science. In fact, it is pretty much the only lesson he remembers from high school (apologies to all my former teachers). Our teacher took us on a field trip to the minor league baseball stadium. Upon arrival we met the head groundskeeper. He taught us why the grass in the stadium was so perfectly maintained and how to get certain colors and looks. He showed us the difference between the soil used on the stadium infield and the dirt most high schools used. He explained the drainage system and why it could rain for an entire day and within two hours the outfield would be completely bone-dry. His presentation was very effective. Never has a group of 9th graders been so interested in grass and dirt. When we got back to school, our teacher asked us to pull out our books to reinforce what we had just learned. Although not every unit began with a trip to the ballpark, this teacher was well known for showing first and telling later.

Create an "I'm Good At" Board

In Chapter 5 we recommended using an "I'm Good At" board. Let's examine this strategy in more detail, using the example of a stressed-out teacher who is tired of her students constantly asking her for help.

At the beginning of the school year, the teacher creates an "I'm Good At" board. Each student brings a self-photo to school and is given two note cards labeled "in school" and "out of school." The students write one thing they are good at in school and one thing they are good at outside school. The pictures and note cards are posted on a large board. Before any student asks the teacher for help, the student consults the "I'm Good At" board. If a fellow classmate is good at the thing the questioning student is struggling with, the questioner is required to ask that classmate for help. If that person is not able to help or is busy working on something else, the student may then ask the teacher.

This method is a great way to help students get to know each other, and it gives them a place to go with questions without constantly nagging the teacher. The "I'm Good At" board is also a great way to hasten the adjustment of new students to the school. They can check the board to see the talents of their classmates and share their own.

Other Teachers and Stress

Educators often ask us how to get cynical teachers who spread negativism to change. Our answer: you can't. We do recommend that all teachers fight cynicism in their school. You can say to a colleague,

"That sounded cynical. Did you mean it that way, or is there a constructive suggestion you have that I missed? Maybe you can say it again in another way so I don't misunderstand you." We can share ideas, collaborate, explain, or show how their life could improve with a willingness to change. That approach might get them to want to change. What *we can insist* on, however, is the banning of toxic talk and actions that can create an extremely negative atmosphere. We all have a right to work in a nontoxic environment. Just as individuals have a right to smoke in their own homes but not in a smoke-free restaurant, teachers who want to complain about or call students names should not be permitted to do so in "public" places like the faculty room and at a staff meeting. We know of one school's faculty room that got so toxic with "anti-everybody" sentiment, most noncomplainers ate alone in their classrooms. Bucking the trend, one brave young teacher sat at an empty table in the faculty room during his lunch hour with a sign reading, "No Trash Talking About Anyone Allowed." Within minutes, that table was half-filled; within a few days, another was added.

Stress and Relationships with Administrators

Relationships with administrators can be a source of stress for many teachers. Here are a few things teachers can do to improve those relationships.

• **Invite them in.** Make it clear that administrators are always welcome to stop in. Some will not take you up on it. If they do, include them in the lesson. Ask them to work individually with a student.

• **Include them during an observation.** Many teachers ask administrators if they "want to be part of an activity." Say instead, "In this room everyone participates. Which group would you like to join, Ms. Principal?" If the administrator protests, do not back down. Remember, inside that classroom the teacher is in charge. It is the teacher's name on the door. If parents are present, they participate as well. Including others gains respect from students and administrators.

• **Explain how your room works.** Let administrators know policies and procedures ahead of time. Show them your social contract before an incident occurs. Show strong leadership and organizational skills. For example, you might tell the principal, "In my room I do my best to be fair to each student, which means I do not always treat them all exactly the same way. I also will not discuss one child with someone else's parent."

• **Tell them you will do your best to handle problems and keep children in class.** We've never met an administrator who wanders the building saying, "Excuse me, I don't see enough of your students. Please send me more because I am not busy enough." Let them know classroom goals and that your number one classroom management strategy is building relationships.

• **Present an alternative rather than a complaint.** We know a principal who says, "You can complain about anything in this school you don't like as long as you have a solution." Administrators are busy. They rarely have time for or interest in hearing people complain. Always come with a solution. If you find yourself continuously referring a student to the office for discipline without seeing improvement, make an appointment and share your thoughts. Here is an example: "Ms. Principal, so far John has not responded with improved behavior following his return from the office. Maybe together we can figure how to better meet his needs." Then listen and offer solutions that might involve you (e.g., "Would you meet with both of us so we can all get clear about what everyone can do differently to get a better result?"). Good administrators will oblige when you present a well-thought-out idea with a proposed solution.

A Tip a Day to Keep Stress in Check

In *The Resilient Teacher,* one of the authors of this book provides daily tips for acquiring and maintaining a positive mind-set (Mendler, 2014). Some of those, as well as some new strategies, are presented here. With approximately 20 school days each month, you can try a different strategy every day.

1. **Take a few deep breaths** intermittently throughout the day. If possible, sit down, close your eyes, and slowly and silently inhale while counting to five. Then exhale to the count of five.

With each inhalation, visualize breathing in fresh, cleansing air. With each exhalation, you rid your body of anger, fear, and stress. Teach students to do this, too. If teaching young children, you can tell them to breathe in big breaths like the dinosaur character Barney and breathe out fire like an angry dragon. Repeat at least a few times. This same strategy can be used to teach students self-control (see p. 156).

2. **Listen to relaxing music.** Many websites provide relaxing music that can help you unwind. Take a few minutes (more if you can) to disconnect from the craziness of the day. Plug in ear buds, close your eyes for a few minutes, and enjoy.

3. **Give before getting.** Have you seen the many televised infomercials offering "free" products and services just for calling? Although these giveaways may include an element of goodwill, clearly the objective is for you to eventually purchase something. Some not-for-profit organizations even send personalized mailing labels along with an invitation to send a contribution. Many car dealers encourage prospective customers to keep a vehicle overnight. Their goal is to get something by giving first. Think of one challenging student who is often stressful and one who is easy to like. For a full day, act toward the challenging student in exactly the same way that you find is natural with the likable student and see what happens.

4. **Bring flowers to the classroom.** Admire and take in their fragrance at least once every half hour. Have students maintain them. If you don't like flowers, bring an object that emits a pleasant aroma and take a few intermittent whiffs throughout the day or whenever your tension begins to rise.

5. **Change the routine.** Most of us stand in the same spot in the classroom or move in a predictable pattern every day without noticing. Every five minutes, teach from a different spot in the room. Occasionally, have students teach part of a lesson.

6. **Take a brisk walk.** Put on comfortable shoes and walk briskly through the halls or outside on the track. Do 10 push-ups in between classes, if you prefer.

7. Keep a "success journal." It seems most people notice when things don't work but rarely when they do. For example, our attention is sparked when we flip a switch and the lights do not turn on. We call the electric company to complain. Rarely do we appreciate when the lights work, and never do most of us even think to write a thank-you letter to the electric company. Even when nothing seems to be going right, there are probably dozens of little things that are. Focus on these; make a list. If doing so seems overwhelming, choose a student who typically adds to your stress and notice all the things that student does well today. Make a list and share it with her toward the end of the day.

8. Bring a picture or two of places or people that give you great joy. Keep it in an easily visible location. Give it a glance every so often. Drift for a few seconds into the picture. Take a moment to relive all the feelings and thoughts you experienced in that place or with that person.

9. Commit to doing less today. Many of us create tension by trying to squeeze too much into each day. Instead of covering two concepts in a lesson, cover one. Instead of running three errands after school, run two. If you are asked to add tasks, politely opt out.

10. Enjoy at least one relaxing meal. Savor every bite and flavor and feel the texture. You work hard. Teaching is a tough profession with little control over most things. You deserve to take good care of yourself.

11. Spend at least 45 minutes having fun. Just as you plan lessons to achieve certain outcomes for students, you can plan activities where the sole outcome is to have fun.

12. Refuse to send a difficult student to the office unless he behaves. You can relieve tension and choose to not reinforce inappropriate student behavior by using the same tone you would use when you are actually telling a student to leave. For example, you might say, "Peter, I see what's going on. You're trying to get removed today. No way! Until I get at least 15 minutes of cooperation from you, you are not going anywhere!"

13. Every Friday, e-mail yourself a list of five specific things that went well that week. Then go home and enjoy the weekend. On Monday morning, read the list.

14. Privately "flip out." When you feel like "flipping out" about somebody or something, imagine the target is present and go ahead and flip out. Yell or scream into a pillow or punch the pillow. Don't hold back. Use any and all words and grunts. When you have finished, look at the situation anew. Clearing your emotions often enables a better understanding of the situation.

15. Go to an open meeting of a recovery organization such as Alcoholics Anonymous or Narcotics Anonymous or to a survivors' support group. Listen to the stories, struggles, and tragedies. Hear how some people have completely changed their lives for the better. It is impossible not to leave feeling grateful.

16. Compliment three students who rarely ignite positive interactions. Go out of your way to interact with them.

17. Ask two top students how you contribute to their success. Say something like, "You are doing very well in this class. I'm very proud and have no doubt you would be doing well with any teacher. Can you tell me what I do that contributes to your success?"

18. Show students and yourself how much control people actually have of their feelings and actions. End class by belly-laughing with your students. First explain that laughter gives the heart and lungs great exercise and is a great way to change a person's mood. Then encourage them to join you in a loud belly laugh that lasts at least 30 seconds. You'll have to force it at first, and so will they. Don't hold back. At the end of the 30 seconds, tell them time is up and to stop laughing. You'll notice that some won't be able to stop—an effect that shows we can change our mood by changing our actions. End by wishing them a happy remainder of the day and reminding them to laugh when they least feel like it.

19. Place an invisible shield around yourself that allows only positive messages in. Watch anything negative bounce off.

20. Reassure yourself. What do you say to a friend who is anxious, worried, upset, or stressed? Most people say, "Don't worry; it's no big deal" or "You'll do better next time" or "Sounds like you said (did) some things you regret. Nobody's perfect." Sometimes they say, "Let's talk it out" or "Tomorrow's a new day." Be kind, forgiving, and reassuring to yourself. Treat yourself as well as you treat your friends.

Final Thoughts

Being a good teacher requires an enormous amount of energy, so take good care of yourself! Follow traditional advice that most of us recite more often than we practice: Eat right and exercise regularly; use calming techniques and other methods of relaxation. You owe this to your students, your family, and yourself. Develop and maintain at least a few favorite outside interests and participate in these no matter how preoccupied or tired you might be. Perhaps most important, keep challenges in perspective by focusing more on what goes right than wrong. Notice and reflect on the positives so troubling events that need further attention are kept in perspective. Be prepared for the roller coaster of life—yours and your students'. Recognize that occasionally you'll have a day when everything goes smoothly; more likely are days when one or more students, parents, or colleagues express some kind of distress; and most probable are days when you experience moments of both. The best thing you can do to keep yourself balanced is to end your workday by reflecting on what went well no matter how small, and plan a strategy or two for a better tomorrow. Then walk out the door and embrace the remainder of the day.

10

Strategies for Students Who Chronically Misbehave

Early in the school year, Mr. Spriggs asked one of the authors to sit in on a conference with his most challenging student. Jon rarely participated appropriately in class, instead drawing attention to himself by "accidentally" dropping books, suddenly having coughing spells, and loudly expelling air from either end. It was considered a relative victory when his disinterest expressed itself more quietly through slouched shoulders, bored yawns, and feigned sleep. As the conference began, Jon seemed prepared for an onslaught of demands and nagging, defending himself with a steely downward glare and arms firmly folded across his chest. Mr. Spriggs opened the conversation by saying,

> Jon, I am really glad you're in my class. I know that it is not your favorite place to be, but I'm trying hard to make sure I'm the right teacher for you. I've tried many different ways to teach you, but so far they haven't worked very well. I'll keep trying so that you learn. That is what is most important to me. I want to thank you for being a part of my class. You are forcing me to be a better teacher, and that is good for me. If you can help me understand what I might be able to do that would make you want to be a better student, I would really like to know that.

Seeming surprised if not shocked by the absence of blame and expected vitriol, Jon appeared to relax and hesitantly offered a few ideas, like not being asked to read aloud and being corrected in private. His suggestions led to an eventual meeting of the minds and vast improvement. Rather than asking or demanding that Jon change, Mr. Spriggs wisely started by opening himself to change. Unlike conventional thinking that might have gone something like "Things between Jon and me would be better if only *he* would [did] _____," his thinking seems to have been more along the lines of "things would be fine between Jon and me if only *I* would [did] _____." Let's look at the *attitudes* reflected by this strategy and the *basic needs* each addresses:

- "I am really glad you're in my class."
    Attitude: Your presence is important to me.
    Basic needs: Attention and connection

- "I've tried many different ways to teach you . . . I'll keep trying."
    Attitude: Not everyone learns the same way.
    Basic need: Competence (success)

- "You are forcing me to be a better teacher."
    Attitude: We can all get better, including me.
    Basic need: Control

- "[What can I] do that would make you want to be a better student?"
    Attitude: I value your opinion.
    Basic need: Identity

Many of the strategies we have already discussed are especially recommended for chronically misbehaving students, but teacher determination and repetition are required. In particular, reframing (which we discussed at length in Chapter 7) is a good place to begin. Is the student "explosive" or "passionate," "defiant" or "independent," "aggressive" or "confident"? The outcome of a problem-solving conference with the student is often influenced by our attitude at the start. For example, if you want to help a student who easily loses control when asked to do something unpleasant, you might reframe in the following way:

You have strong feelings when you are told to do things you don't like. I see that especially when I ask you to read. I nag you about that because I worry that if you don't practice, school is going to get harder and harder. As you get older, you'll be expected to do more and more reading. I have some ideas about how you could push away those "I don't want to read" feelings before they get you upset. Would you like to know what they are?

Many different kinds of interventions can help turn things around with students who chronically misbehave. These include exploratory questions that are designed to promote reflection and insight, and negotiation strategies in which student and teacher (sometimes with the involvement of one or more resource personnel, teachers, or parents) find ways to make life more acceptable for everyone. Other interventions with more of an instructional focus aim to teach students improved social, problem-solving, impulse control, and self-regulation skills. A few include traditional behavior modification techniques that can help teach more appropriate behaviors (although they should be used only as a last resort), and others are unconventional approaches that rely on elements such as role-reversal, humor, and paradox.

Exploratory Questions

Exploratory questions are designed for the teacher to ask students when things are stable, to promote reflection and insight that may lead to a better future plan. Here are some examples:

- What can you tell me about the behavior that upset me so much?
- Do you know you are [name the behavior] when you are doing it?
- Do you know why we have a rule about [behavior]?
- Can you stop [behavior] when you want to stop?
- Can you stop [behavior] when you are asked to stop?
- Who is usually best able to get you to control your behavior? What does she do? How might you begin doing that yourself?

- What do you think would happen if everyone [behavior]?
- If you were in charge, what would you do if someone kept breaking this rule? How do you think that would help?

Negotiation Strategies

Students who continually misbehave often need individualized help to learn how to follow the classroom rules. Some respond well with efforts to elicit their cooperation through negotiation. Positive student confrontation and the family intervention process are two negotiation methods to consider.

Positive Student Confrontation

Positive student confrontation is a mediation process that involves setting aside time to meet individually with a student in an attempt to resolve differences by negotiating. It is a time-consuming process; thus, it is best done with students whose misbehavior takes up excessive class time. For this approach to be effective, teachers must be willing to view the misbehavior as a symptom of a conflict between teacher and student, listen to a student's complaints or concerns, and show some degree of flexibility. The idea is to find solutions that are good for both sides.

Although a meeting or a series of meetings between the teacher and student can be sufficient, it is usually best to involve a *neutral* third person who can guide both parties to find common ground that can make things better for each. This person may be another teacher, a counselor, an administrator, a resource person, or even another student. The important attributes of the third person are being a good listener, not getting actively involved in the negotiation, and being able to remain calm when the going gets rough. We refer to this mediator as a "coach."

The process includes the teacher and student taking turns telling each other their dislikes, likes, and wants related to the misbehavior. After each step, the coach repeats the statement to ensure understanding. Once all of the information is presented, solutions are sought. When a plan of action is determined, the teacher and student are asked to sign an individual contract, and another meeting is scheduled to check how well the plan is working.

Individual negotiation requires the aggrieved teacher to be willing to

- Share directly with the student.
- Risk hearing unpleasant things from the student.
- Consider program modifications for the student.

It also comes with the fundamental belief that student opinions, ideas, and thoughts are important and will be valued, listened to, and even acted on in this classroom. Before positive student confrontation begins, it can be extremely helpful for the coach to discuss the process with each party separately so each knows what to expect. The specific guidelines for positive student confrontation are as follows.

1. The coach (third party) describes the problem, process, and his or her role. For example, the coach may say, "I understand there are some things going on in the classroom that are making it hard for you, Mrs. Jones, to teach, and hard for you, Joe, to follow the rules. I'm here to see if we can find some ways for each of you to feel better and cooperate in class."

2. The coach encourages both the teacher and student to share feelings of dislike, resentment, anger, or frustration. For example, the coach may say to the teacher, "This may not be easy, but tell Joe what he says or does that makes it hard for you to teach." After the teacher responds, the coach then addresses the student. For example, the coach might ask, "What goes on in the classroom that makes it hard for you to follow the rules?" After each side has a turn, each is encouraged to repeat or paraphrase the other's statements; this helps ensure an understanding of concerns ("Joe, what did Mrs. Jones just say about you, and what makes it hard for her to teach?"; "Mrs. Jones, what did Joe just say about the class, and what makes it hard for him to follow the rules?"). Be aware that when asked to paraphrase, the person at the receiving end often denies the other person's allegation or becomes defensive. When that happens, it is important for the coach to reassure the listener that agreement is not essential ("You don't have to agree with Ms. Jones. For now, just repeat what she thinks you do that makes it hard for her to teach." (Paraphrasing applies to subsequent steps as well.)

3. The teacher and student share appreciations. ("Tell what you like or appreciate about Mrs. Jones.")

4. The teacher and student make demands. ("Tell what you want Joe to do differently from what he is doing right now.")

5. The teacher and student negotiate a solution. ("Tell what you are willing to do differently that you think can help solve this problem.")

6. Agreement is reached, put in writing, and signed.

7. Evaluation responsibilities are established so that each side can keep track of how well the agreement is working.

8. A follow-up meeting is scheduled.

The coach needs to be aware that both sides usually come with a list of complaints that feed their frustrations. It is important in these cases that the coach ask the teacher and student to list only the two or three things that they most want to see changed. This keeps the process manageable for all involved. If by the end of a session both sides can agree to make small but clear changes, that success can be used as a building block to pave the way toward resolving other concerns.

Family Intervention

The family intervention process is a collaborative effort among school personnel, parents, and the student to define concrete and reachable goals and positive or negative consequences contingent on goal attainment. Goals must be specific, measurable, and reachable. The steps are as follows.

1. Meet with parent(s). Begin with either a two-part meeting or two separate ones. If the child lives in a two-parent home, strongly request a meeting with both parents. If the student is living with a single parent, then meet alone or include any and all extended family or live-in adults who frequently contribute to child-rearing. For the first part of the meeting, it is best not to have the student involved so you and the parents can talk freely and come to agreement on working as a team. Children are often skilled at manipulating the teacher and parents to work against rather than with each other. Point out to the parents the negative consequences for continued inappropriate behavior. (The best one is that their child will likely choose friends who influence further negative behavior. All parents worry about their children's friends.) Others include poor grades, less options for the future, labeling that stays with the child, or developing an attitude of self-failure.

2. **Be certain that the problem is lack of effort.** For example, make sure you know the student has the ability to perform the behavior but is choosing not to. Decide which problem to tackle first. Because this is a powerful intervention, asking the child to reach an unattainable goal will only make things much worse. Be sure to stress that you want to help the child be more successful. Do not blame. Say things like "I want the student to

"Participate in class activities."

"Stop hitting or pushing other students."

"Stay awake in class."

"Be on time."

"Stop hurting other students' feelings."

3. **Agree together on a concrete goal that is measurable and can be reached in a short amount of time.** In the second part of the meeting, the student should be present. Invite all participants to be active in reaching an agreement on a specific goal for the student—for example, completing at least 80 percent of the next two homework assignments. Vague goals, like "less interrupting" or "stop instigating trouble," don't work because the student may think she has accomplished the goal whereas the teacher may not. "Be on time to class at least three days next week" is an example of a clear goal.

4. Establish positive and negative consequences for reaching or failing to reach the goal. The student and parents are important partners in identifying what these consequences are and when they will be implemented. Use positive consequences that are not material. One of the best is spending time with a person of choice. Often students choose fathers, because many children spend less time with their fathers than they would like. It can help to plan a specific activity with the person of choice. Be careful not to promise more than can be delivered. It's better to promise an hour of playing a favorite game and to follow through than to promise three hours and give only two. The student must believe he received what was agreed to.

The negative consequence can be the temporary loss of something the student enjoys, like smartphone time. Encourage the parents and child to negotiate both the activity to be curtailed and the amount of time. Be sure the negative consequence is reasonable enough for the parents to carry out. Losing the use of a smartphone for one night is better than agreeing on five nights but letting the student off the hook after two.

5. Consider making the plan a written contract in which the student says what she agrees to do, what she will receive if successful, and what she will lose if unsuccessful.

6. Decide how you will monitor the student's progress and what kinds of follow-up will be done (e.g., sending home daily or weekly reports; setting a date for the next meeting).

Teaching and Practicing Key Social Skills

Teachers often assume that all children know basic social skills, but many don't—particularly those who frequently get into trouble. Because children often imitate their parents, they may learn negative behavior from parents who lack social skills.

Persistence is necessary in teaching social skills because chronically misbehaving students are often locked into behaviors that have become automatic but are inappropriate in a school setting. Virtually all teachers can teach most of these strategies informally without requiring a curriculum. Many of the skills described here can also be shared as components of classroom procedures. Just as athletic coaches and directors of school plays know the value of practice repetitions for mastering skills under real conditions, the same is true for social skills, especially if these skills are not a regular part of home life. Students respond best in a trusting atmosphere because they are learning and practicing skills that often take time to master.

It is beyond the scope of this book to offer a curriculum on social skills training. Many solid programs are available (e.g., the Tennessee Behavior Supports Project [https://etbsp.utk.edu] and resources from Goldstein, 1999; Henley, 2003; Lane, Kalberg, & Menzies, 2009). Instead, we offer tips on social skills that we know are especially necessary and are frequently lacking among students who chronically misbehave.

Basic Social Skills

• **Greeting others.** Troubled children rarely say, "Good morning," "Nice to see you," "Hi," or "Have a nice day." Instead of complaining about their bad manners, we advocate teaching them these skills.

• **Showing eye contact.** Children with poor social skills need practice making eye contact—even those from cultures that consider eye contact to be a negative behavior (including many Asians and Native Americans). Such children can benefit from learning that eye contact with certain people can help them get what they need in the larger culture. Of course, we must be sensitive to the cultural component while simultaneously exploring where, when, and with whom this skill can be beneficial.

• **Making a request.** Teach children to start a request with "Please" or "I would appreciate." Also remind them to close a request with "Thank you."

• **Getting someone's attention.** This skill is best achieved with words like "Excuse me" or "I'd like to tell you what I think."

• **Following instructions.** Share with your students that before they do something, they need to listen to directions. Then they need to repeat back each step of the directions before doing the task.

- **Accepting criticism.** This social skill is about students learning they do not have to argue or deny when somebody says something critical. They can simply say, "Thanks for the feedback" and either accept or dismiss it.

- **Resisting peer pressure.** Here are a few easy lines students can learn to use when they do not want to join in but are feeling pressured:

> "I don't enjoy doing things like that, but I hope you have a good time."

> "Let me know how it goes."

> "Let's try _____ instead. It's even more fun [scary, challenging, goofy] than your idea."

How to Disagree Without Being Disagreeable

Disagreeing without being disagreeable is a social skill that many students lack. A common manifestation of this problem is the choice of words used to express a different point of view. Although there are many reasons for this problem, learning to listen to someone with a different point of view and then responding respectfully is an important life skill for students to learn, as well as a vital element in a well-managed classroom.

Teach students how to appropriately disagree with you and each other. What do you want your students to say or do when they have a different point of view? Do they know the difference between giving an opinion that offers a different point of view and one that does little more than criticize? Teach them to paraphrase before sharing: "So as you see it, _____"; "What you're saying is _____."

It is extremely important that students learn how to disagree with a value or an idea without attacking a person. For example, you may tell them: "It is not helpful to call each other stupid, laugh, roll your eyes, or use put-downs when you don't agree with what someone says or does. You can either not comment or offer your opinion and explain why you see things differently without attacking the other person." Let students know that the way to disagree is to say, "I don't see it that way," "I disagree," or "My opinion is," followed by whatever the reason might be. If you hear inappropriate comments, challenge and correct the student ("That was a put-down. Can you say that again by telling how your opinion is different from mine?").

Identify and express enthusiasm when you see or hear your students respectfully disagreeing; for example, "I am really impressed! That was a fantastic discussion, especially when Morgan and Sue—who have very different beliefs about legalizing marijuana—were able to calmly present these views without attacking each other. I think politicians could learn a lot from you!"

Self-Control Strategies

All the strategies described here involve students trying new thoughts or behaviors, and they require sufficient practice so that the strategies become automatic responses to self-control issues; otherwise their shelf life will be very short. Students with poor self-control are often hypersensitive to criticism. They need to learn and practice how to calm themselves and then choose how they want to handle a difficult situation. The following activities are designed to teach students how to do that.

Calming Techniques

Here are three techniques you can teach your students to help them calm down in difficult situations.

1. Change thoughts and images. Teach students that before they react, it can help to imagine that somebody said or did something that wouldn't bother them at all. Ask your students one, both, or a variation of these questions:

"If somebody called you a book, a cup, or a chair, how would you react?"

"If someone who laughed or smirked at you when you made a mistake had his shoes on the wrong feet and ink dripping down the side of his mouth, how would you feel?"

In the discussion that follows, students will usually say there was something wrong with that person, and they would likely not get mad or feel upset. Teach your students that when they hear hurtful words or gestures, before they say or do anything, they should pretend that the speaker said one or more ridiculous things instead. Or ask them to picture someone calling them a name but dressed like a clown with a big bug crawling on his head. Point out that we all have power to control our feelings by adjusting our thoughts and images.

2. **Take a few deep breaths.** Teach your students to take a few deep breaths when they feel angry or scared. Have them practice counting silently to 5 or 10 with their eyes closed while inhaling and doing the same as they exhale. Suggest they breathe in calm, relaxing, fresh air and breathe out any anger or fear they may feel. Young students can breathe in big breaths like the dinosaur character Barney and breathe out fire like an angry dragon. Repeat this at least a few times.

3. **Focus on positive thoughts.** It has been known for some time that what we think strongly affects how we feel. Most adults are fully aware of this connection. Children are not. Use their experiences to teach them this connection. For example, you might ask them to think about a TV show they really like watching. Then ask them how they feel while they are thinking about the show. How do they feel when they think about their favorite toy, place to visit, or food? Then connect how positive thoughts can help when bad things happen, like somebody saying something mean. Share and explore specific positive thoughts that they can use to remind themselves of their good qualities when somebody is trying to get them upset. Here are some examples:

"I am a good person and I won't let _____ make me feel bad."

"I am smart."

"I am able to do lots of things."

"I will not allow anyone to make me feel bad."

"I don't have to agree with the bad things some other students say about me. Nobody is perfect. I can remind myself of the good things."

"If someone bothers me, I will let it bounce off me like I bounce on a trampoline."

Thinking Before Acting to Avoid and Solve Problems

Most successful students learn to quietly verbalize what they think, and they use these verbalizations to guide their academic and social behaviors. In their own minds, they are able to say such things as "I need to raise my hand" so they do not blurt out, and "I'm mad right now, but if I hit her I'll get into trouble, and that isn't worth it." By contrast, students in frequent trouble need specific help learning how to anticipate problem situations and then practice what to say or do. For example, in an early social skills program (Camp, Blom, Herbert, & Van Doorninck, 1977) whose elements have been incorporated in later ones (e.g., the Tennessee Behavior Supports Project; see also Mendler, 2005, 2012), students are taught to think aloud and problem-solve, using these questions:

1. What is my problem?
2. What is my plan to solve the problem?
3. Am I using my plan?
4. How did I do?

The problem-solving approach first developed by Meichenbaum (1977) includes the following questions and statements:

1. What am I supposed to do?
2. I need to look at all possibilities.
3. I have to focus and concentrate.
4. I have to make a choice.
5. How well did I do?

Adolescent Anger Control

In techniques for adolescent anger control developed by Feindler and Ecton (1986), the student takes these steps:

1. Identify direct (provocations by another person) and indirect (thinking someone is being unfair or lying) anger triggers.
2. Identify physiological states related to anger (e.g., getting hot, sweating, clenching hands, tightening facial muscles).

3. Practice relaxation methods (e.g., counting backward, taking deep breaths, taking a walk).

4. Use cognitive-behavioral methods (e.g., reminders such as "Chill out," "Take it easy," "Just stay calm," or "It's not worth the hassle").

5. Conduct an evaluation, asking yourself, "How did I do?" (e.g., "I did well"; "I kept in control"; "I did OK"; "I felt like killing him, and I only said ____. I can do even better next time"; "I lost it. Next time this happens, I'll need to remind myself to ____.").

Reminders Through Acronyms

Many people remember the names of the Great Lakes through the acronym HOMES (Huron, Ontario, Michigan, Erie, Superior). Students can use acronyms as well to more easily and quickly remember the steps involved in maintaining self-control when problems occur. Here are some examples:

STOMA:
Stop before you do anything.
Take a breath; then think about what happened and what you want to do.
Options: What are the consequences of each choice?
Move on it (make a choice).
Appreciate yourself (for not losing control and doing your best).

WIN:
What is the problem?
Identify possible solutions.
Narrow it down to the best choice.

TAG:
Tell others what they are doing to bother you.
Ask them to stop.
Go tell someone if they do not.

QTIP: Quit **T**aking **I**t **P**ersonally
STAR: Stop; **T**hink; **A**ct; **R**eview

Two Powerful Questions

You can also teach self-control by asking your students these questions:

1. What do people say or do that makes you feel mad?
2. Why do you think people say or do these things?

The first question elicits many spontaneous responses from students, such as "When others do not share," "Name-calling," "Taking my stuff," and "Calling my mama names." It is usually best for the teacher to list these responses and then guide discussion to the second question, varying the next question depending on the age of the student:

With older students: "When others say or do these things, are they trying to *give you power,* or are they trying to *rob you of your power?*"

With younger students: "Are they trying to make you feel weak or strong?"

With very young children: "Are they trying to make you feel happy or sad?"

Follow this by asking, "Do you want to give them the power to [get you in a conflict with me or the principal; feel weak; be unhappy]?" Finally, brainstorm, present, or teach strategies that can help students find ways of handling these types of difficult situations without getting into trouble. You might introduce assertion strategies from the next section as examples.

Assertion Techniques

Teaching students to substitute *assertive* behavior for *aggressive* behavior can be a turning point in gaining feelings of control and power. Strategies need to be taught and practiced so students can master these techniques.

Walking Away Assertively

We especially recommend practicing this technique because it is much easier said than done. Express understanding of how the desire for respect and the need for pride can make it difficult to walk away. Frame walking away as a skill to keep our own power so that we do not give power away to someone who wants to make us feel bad. Teachers then need to model this approach when they are in a situation that requires walking away.

Here is an illustration of a strategy to make walking away more palatable:

Teacher (privately to Erin): If I call you a pencil, are you a pencil?

Erin: No.

Teacher: What are you?

Erin: A girl.

Teacher: If I call you a book, does that mean you are a book?

Erin: No.

Teacher: What are you?

Erin: A girl.

Teacher: If someone calls you a baby, are you a baby?

Erin: No.

Teacher: What are you?

Erin: A girl.

Teacher: Can you walk away from someone who cannot tell the difference between a girl and a baby?

I-Messages

Students can use I-messages to assert themselves with other students and with their teacher. It is usually enough to say, "I do not like it when ____. Please stop." Then walk away.

The Bother/Want Strategy

This strategy teaches students to say what bothers them and what they want. For example: "It *bothers* me when you push me. I *want* you to stop."

Escalated Assertion

You can teach students to use gradually intensifying statements as an appropriate way to get what they want without getting into trouble. Here's an example:

"Please give me my book back."

"I asked you to give me my book back."

"I know you want that book, but it belongs to me, and I want it back."

"If I don't get my book back, we'll probably both get into trouble, so thanks for giving it back."

"Hassling with you over the book isn't worth it" (walks away and worries about the book later).

Quick Comebacks

Prepare students with easy-to-learn responses they can use when somebody is picking on them or trying to bait them into an argument. Here are a few examples:

"I'm sorry you feel that way."

"How can I help you see things differently?"

"I don't agree, but if you want to believe that, go ahead."

"I wish you felt differently."

"That is your opinion and you are free to have it, just as I am to reject it."

"I'm sorry if I did something to make you mad."

Behavior Modification

When choosing rewards, you must first decide if the benefits are worth the cost (see p. 34). Behavior modification may change behavior, but it also reduces self-control. Rewards are addictive, and it is often hard to remove them. Have you ever heard a child say, "I demand you give me less?" It's more likely that you hear "Is that all?"

Behavior modification should only be a last resort to serious problems. It is best used for children who have little chance of independent living in their future or children with serious behavioral or emotional issues. In spite of the problems it can cause, behavior modification, when used in controlled settings, is a strategy that benefits children with special challenges and cannot be dismissed.

Daily Rating Cards

You can use a daily student rating card (see Figure 10.1) to rate and monitor agreed-upon behavior established through one of the negotiation strategies. You can also use the rating card on its own. On the card, the day is arranged by class period or subject, and the student

Figure 10.1
Daily Rating Card

Student's name _____ Date _____

Please rate this student in each of the areas listed below using ratings of 1 to 4.

1 = Excellent   2 = Good   3 = Fair   4 = Poor

Area	Class Period/Subject						Comments
	1	2	3	4	5	6	
Classroom participation							
Cooperation							
Class assignments							
Homework							
Peer interaction							

1 = 5 points   2 = 3 points   3 = 1 point   4 = 0 points

Source: From "80+ Accommodations for Children or Teens with AD/HD," by R. A. Barkley, 2014, *The ADHD Report, 16*(4), 7–10. Copyright 2014 by Guilford Press. Available: https://robinbillings.files.wordpress.com/2014/04/80classroomaccommodations.pdf

is rated in relevant categories. Each rating is associated with a certain number of points that can be accumulated. The ratings are tallied, and positive or negative consequences are implemented either at home or at school. You can find numerous online templates of behavior cards for students of all grade levels that can be easily downloaded for use. You should not use rating cards publicly.

At the beginning of the program or as the student shows improvement, the responsibility for rating and selection of a consequence is either shared with or given to the student. For example, after a period of relative compliance requiring close teacher monitoring, the next step is to give the student an opportunity to do her own ratings while you do yours. Next, the student does her own ratings independently after a period of relative agreement between the teacher's ratings and her own. Finally, the program is discontinued because the behavior has been internalized and the student "graduates."

Teaching Students How to Use Positive Reinforcement

Students who often get into trouble are usually unaware of the power they have to change how teachers react to them. If you work with individuals or small groups of behaviorally challenging students, teach them basic principles of behavior modification, especially how to use "positive reinforcement" if they complain or blame their teachers.

We know a guidance counselor who teaches some of her students "Ways to Con Your Teacher." Among the ways are the following:

- Look at the teacher when he or she is speaking.
- In class, call or use the teacher's name at least once a day when you talk to him or her.
- Arrive early, smile at your teacher, and say "hi."
- When a teacher gives you a suggestion or corrects your errors, say "thank you."
- If a teacher corrects your behavior, say "I'm sorry."
- Make one good comment in class each day.
- Do your homework and turn it in on time.
- Do not make unnecessary noises like talking when the teacher is talking, humming, drumming on your desk, tapping your pencil, or pounding your feet.

- If you have trouble staying in your seat, tell your teacher and ask for suggestions.
- If you do not understand something, ask the teacher to explain it differently using other words or examples.
- At the end of class, tell the teacher one thing he or she did that you liked.
- Thank the teacher for teaching a good lesson.

If you are a guidance counselor, it is important to let teachers know that you are trying to get the student to act more appropriately and will be teaching these strategies. Otherwise, teachers may at first react negatively to what they may perceive as disingenuous comments from the student. Tell them to initially expect the student to seem awkward, because these are new behaviors.

Unconventional Strategies

Teachers often relate to challenging students in very predictable ways: they give up, or they use threats, rewards, or punishment. The main purpose of an unconventional strategy is to interrupt the flow of disruptive behavior by saying and doing things that force the student to find new ways of fulfilling the needs for connection and control. Because these strategies are purposely designed to confuse the student into developing new patterns of behavior and interaction, they are initially outside most teachers' comfort zone and usually require considerable practice before using. Most of them serve the same purpose as the informal methods discussed in Chapter 7, except these are most appropriate for especially challenging students when more conventional methods just don't work.

Legitimize the Problem Behavior

Teacher opposition to problem behavior is the fuel that feeds many students who chronically misbehave. The more we object, criticize, blame, and punish, the stronger the undesirable behavior becomes. Implementing ways to unemotionally channel the behavior can be much more successful. When behavior occurs excessively, we have a better chance of ending it when we allow it but limit it. For example, it can be wise to permit five minutes of "social time" for a class that is endlessly chatting or an opportunity for the class clown to tell his three best jokes every day.

To begin this approach, either gather data or estimate how often the unacceptable behavior is occurring on average. Then allow for a number that is more than you'd normally accept but considerably lower than average. In some cases, you can negotiate the number with the student or class. For example, if a student is shouting out 20 times each day, tell him that you can't live with that number because it's too disruptive, and you'd rather not have any but could probably live with as many as 5. Then say, "Give me a number that could work for you." If the number is too large, negotiate downward until you find a number comfortable for both of you.

Use Coupons to Legitimize

Except for aggressive behaviors that can be harmful to others, you can use coupons to manage excessive behaviors you find objectionable. Give a targeted student a limited number of coupons that allow her to perform the very behavior she already does excessively. For example, you might give a student who constantly complains five "complaint coupons" (initially the number of coupons should be close to but less than what is done on average). At a relatively private moment, you can say something like this:

> Jenny, you have a lot of ideas about how to make the class better. At the same time, it's hard for me to listen as much as I would like several times a day. So I'm giving you four complaint coupons to use. Just give me a coupon each time you're going to say something you don't like about the class or have a suggestion about how to make it better.

This approach can be used for many types of behaviors—talking out of turn, making excuses, tapping a pencil, not doing homework, getting out of one's seat, and so forth. See Figure 10.2 for an example of a complaint coupon.

Figure 10.2
Example of a Behavior Coupon

Reverse Roles

Many teachers have used the technique of allowing a student to play teacher for a short time. This strategy is designed to carry that concept one step further. If a student is making it difficult for you to teach, give him the responsibility of teaching your class for a significant time period. For example, you might say, "Lou, I can't teach when you shout, and I am sure you can do a better job than me. Let's trade places. Anything other than 'class dismissed' [identify other limits if you have them] would be fine."

Most students will hesitate to be in charge and will back off, usually stopping their inappropriate behavior. When they do, simply resume teaching. It is common for students to save face by making an inappropriate comment (e.g., "Whatever") or doing something unacceptable. If you let that be the "last word," the method usually works very well. If they do take over, sit in a different seat but otherwise act at least as badly as the student usually does. Make it virtually impossible for the student to assume control. Most students stop after a very brief period. Some might actually continue. A few may do a decent job teaching.

After the experience, meet privately with the student to try to solve your conflicts. Some students are amazed to see a mirror image (or worse) of how they usually behave. This approach can open the door to developing a plan or contract for improved decision making.

Use Humor and Nonsense

Write down various jokes, phrases, sayings, and statements that you find funny or nonsensical. Try to include in your list some that are certain to get a reaction from many of your students. At least once a day for one week, when a student behaves disruptively, respond with one of your funny statements. For example, as Nate comes to class late for the third day in a row, tell him poetically, "Nate! Nate! You're late, mate. When you're tardy, you're missing the party."

We have long known that humor is a characteristic often noted among teachers who have excellent rapport with their students (Loomans & Kolberg, 2002; Lundberg & Thurston, 2002). More than 40 years ago, Moscowitz and Hayman (1974) found that those teachers rated "best" by inner-city high school students used more humor than did those rated "typical."

Agree with the Put-Down, Criticism, or Accusation

You can deflect many inappropriate and even nasty comments by agreeing that there is some truth in the accusation and then redirecting the conversation. For example, Joe says the lesson is stupid. Instead of arguing, the teacher says, "You might be right." It is important to train yourself to hear loaded comments with the same emotion that you would feel if someone called you something neutral or something silly, like a chair. This makes it much easier to think of a nonaggressive way to defuse a potential power struggle.

Answer Improbably

Imagine telling a student that you've had enough of his behavior and you offer him the option to either stop or leave. He looks you square in the eye in the middle of class and says he's not going, you can't make him stop, and "What are you going to do about it?" Imagine saying, "I'm going to finish this lesson, hop over to the airport, and take the first flight to Mars!" How do you suppose he and the other students might react? A teacher we know whose student called her a "motherfucker" calmly responded, "At least you got it half right." A student asked another teacher why he had to "learn this dumb junk." Her answer was "One, the school district and state say I have to teach it; two, here is their phone number—when you know why we have to do it, please tell us all!"

Behave Paradoxically

Behaving paradoxically is based on the idea (Frankl, 1963/2006) that people tend to resist change when they feel forced to let go of the familiar. Think of a stubborn man who knows he drinks too much; he is likely to drink even more when nagged to stop by his concerned wife. A young oppositional child who is firmly told to stop throwing a toy is likely to throw it again. Paradoxically, it is almost always more effective to pretend to be angry while telling the child that he'd better keep throwing the toy. Most children stop. Similarly, many of the most challenging students exert lots of energy to continue their inappropriate behavior in the face of threats and punishments. Students who are defiant want to do anything other than what the teacher wants. If the teacher tells a student who refuses to sit, "Do not sit down," the student either has to obey the teacher or defy him by doing what the teacher wants.

Consider the following typical and paradoxical messages:

Typical: "Jane, I will tolerate no more swearing in this class. If you use those words again, you are out of here!"

Paradoxical: "Jane, you said 'bull*shit*.' I think you meant to say 'bull *feces*.' Let's hear it again, except this time with the proper term."

The paradoxical method can be the first step in the *two-step intervention* (see Chapter 7). Follow up later, when things have calmed down. In your follow-up, try saying something such as this: "Carmen, when you get defiant like you did today, I'm not sure what you need from me. If you can just tell me what you really need, I'll help the best I can, and we can both win."

One way to think paradoxically is to incorporate reframing. Imagine that what the student is trying to do is acceptable, but the way he does it is inappropriate. Here's an example: "Henry, you are very strong-willed when you don't want to do something. In a lot of situations, like someone telling you to take drugs, it's great to say no. So I know I can't make you do the work if you don't want to; but when you don't, it is impossible for me to know if you're learning what I'm teaching. That said, if you feel strongly that doing this work is against your values and will make you a bad person, then don't do it. I'll leave it to you do decide."

There are situations in which we would not advise this technique in a school setting. The most obvious involve fighting or hard hitting (as opposed to the playful shoving that many middle school students use to express friendship and camaraderie). As well, due to their difficulty in reading social nuance and a tendency to interpret what is said literally, it is best to avoid using this strategy with autistic students.

Although a hint of humor may be appropriate, avoid sarcasm when using a paradoxical method. It works only when you convey your genuine belief that the only one with the real power to effect change is the student.

Use Nonverbal Messages

Students who chronically misbehave have been verbally reprimanded thousands of times before. They eventually become immune to verbal messages, which they tune out. Try using prearranged nonverbal signals to cue students to the fact that you've had enough. It can be any mutually prearranged signal such as a facial expression or a gesture.

Throw a Good Old-Fashioned Tantrum

Every so often, probably no more than two or three times a year, a well-timed tantrum in which you might yell, scream, stand on chairs, or even knock over a table or two can be wonderfully refreshing and renewing. It reminds students that you, like all humans, have your limits and that there are times you care deeply enough about your students to respond with visceral, nonviolent, but poignant, gut-releasing emotion. Although you will be reacting emotionally, be sure to throw a tantrum only when you are in control and have decided that this issue is worth it. Don't impulsively react this way, because you are likely to say or do something you may well regret. Just remember, doing this every day makes you look like a lunatic, so be extremely selective. This strategy should not be used with emotionally fragile or autistic students due to their difficulty in adapting to and recovering from the unexpected.

Record Your Class or Specific Students

Some students are committed to denying all responsibility for being disruptive. Furthermore, a phone call home may be greeted with a parent defending his child's actions. When you are confronted with such a situation, it can be helpful to tell the student, "Beginning today, I will be recording our class time. Because I think it's important for both you and your parents to understand the problems that we have here, the recording will be available to your parents when we meet to discuss your school progress."

This method has been extremely effective in curtailing a wide range of inappropriate behaviors (especially verbal abuse, put-downs, and swearing). Be aware of the "cosmetic effect," however. When people first see or hear themselves, they frequently pay more attention to how they look or sound than to what they are doing. It might take three or four times before students can actually benefit from viewing or hearing themselves.

Focus on those students who give you the most difficulty. Discuss their feelings about the way they looked or sounded. Explore the need for change. When given a chance to actually see or hear themselves, students often gain an awareness of how they come off and are willing to try something new. Naturally, check with administration before recording to make sure no school policies or state laws prohibit this practice.

Put Students in Charge of Their Own Problem

Because many students who misbehave are trying to feel in control, look for ways to put them in charge of moments that can be problematic. For example, students who have trouble getting from one place to the next can be put in charge of making sure everyone behaves on the way. The playground bully can be empowered to look after others to make sure there is no teasing or taunting. The student who is constantly out of her seat can be asked to plan or lead some movement exercises and activities for the entire class. On a more regular basis, many students with control issues benefit from being helpers or mentors (e.g., pairing older students with younger ones).

Use Exercise Regularly

A growing body of data suggests exercise as a treatment for ADHD; it may even be an effective replacement for medication for some students (Wendt, 2002). Jensen (2000) advocates exercise as an effective intervention with students who fit at least 5 different categories of disorders (out of 10 addressed in his book). Among many others recently, Wilson and Conyers (2013) and Ratey (2013) have reported numerous academic and behavioral benefits of movement. It seems like nearly every day there is a newspaper article or a blog reporting the positive impact of exercise on some aspect of learning and behavior.

Introduce movement activities often in your classroom. For every 8 to 10 minutes of listening, try to think of a 1- or 2-minute activity that requires at least some movement. This can be as simple as sharing an idea with someone, doing a "finding someone who" activity, or doing a think-pair-share. We know a behavior intervention specialist who has a small trampoline in her office for use by children who are too out of control to talk. As they bounce up and down (which reduces their excess energy), they begin to talk through what happened.

Solicit Ideas from Colleagues

Too often in schools, we underutilize each other when it comes to borrowing potentially helpful ideas. Write out a situation or problem you face and omit the ending—as in a mystery puzzle. Distribute copies to any of your colleagues you trust or who you feel have a good reputation for dealing with difficult students. Include an administrator and one or two resource personnel, such as the school psychologist. Have each of them write in their ending or describe how they would handle the situation. Ask them to be specific.

Implement an Attitude-Change Strategy

It is not unusual to think that if only others changed their ways, our lives would be so much better. For example, we might think, "If only my students cared about their work, teaching would be great. If only I got more support from the administration [or parents or district or state education department], things would be so much better." Although there is nothing wrong with trying to improve our circumstances, as we all know, the only real control we ultimately have is over what we do and how we do it.

Try this experiment (Curwin, 2010):

1. Make a list of five or more things that would make you happier and better as a teacher. For example:
    - Give fewer formal tests.
    - Have more supplies.
    - Have fewer discipline problems.
    - Have more parent support.
    - Allow more time for myself during the day.

2. Ask yourself which of the items on your list you can control, partially control, or have no control over.

3. Figure out how to live with those you can't control (e.g., testing).

4. Take control of what you can control (e.g., find an hour for yourself by rearranging your priorities and schedule).

5. Change the way you respond to items you partially control (e.g., working with parents).

We are much more likely to influence change in others when we treat them as we want them to be rather than as they are. So for the next two or three weeks, try the following experiment (Mendler, 2014), which will require some tweaking of your attitude and behavior.

Start by thinking about your most challenging student (or class). How do you feel about this student, and how do you act? What comments or adjectives come naturally? Now think of your best-behaved or highest-achieving student (or class). How do you feel about this student, and how do you act? When you think about this student, what comments come naturally? When this student makes a mistake, how do you usually react? When you see this student's parent, what do you say? For the next two weeks, act toward your worst-behaved or lowest-performing student in the same way you would your best student. Greet him the same way. Use the same kinds of encouraging language that you might with your high-performing student. Treat him as if he has already achieved the same level of performance or behavior as your best-behaved or best-performing student, even if he only completed 1 problem out of 10. Bring the same degree of energy and pride to the relationship. Try not to be dissuaded by what the student actually says or does. In fact, at those times try to focus on how his challenging behavior is helping to make you a better teacher. See what happens.

11

Special Challenges

The U.S. Centers for Disease Control and Prevention (2016) estimate that 1 in 68 children has an autism-spectrum disorder. In 2006, the prevalence was 1 in 110. Although attention deficit hyperactivity disorder (ADHD) has been known for decades, an ever-growing number of students are being diagnosed. Estimates range from 5 percent of children (American Psychiatric Association, 2013) to 11 percent of children ages 4 to 17 (Visser et al., 2014).

Although medication can be of benefit behaviorally and possibly academically, some students don't respond to medication, whereas others who show many symptoms are never formally diagnosed and therefore have never had medication prescribed. Many of these students who have a difficult time with attention and concentration can also be disruptive in the classroom because they may often get out of their seats, talk incessantly, make noises, fidget, and have unmet sensory needs.

In addition to students with special needs, we address two other challenges in this chapter: how to interact effectively with belligerent and enabling parents who either create behavior problems in their children or add fuel to the fire, and how to interrupt the "school-to-prison pipeline" too often seen among impoverished youth and largely concentrated in the inner city. Although these issues defy simple solutions, this chapter offers practical ways to address them.

Students with Special Needs

We recently met a teacher who complained about a 2nd grade student who didn't pay attention. When asked for an example, she replied, "When he ties his shoe, he knocks everything off his desk. By the time he picks everything up, his shoe is untied again, and it starts all over. He hums in a low tone and occasionally cruises around the room." When asked if he had the correct answer when called upon, she answered, "He always knows the right answer." The real problem, then, was that he paid attention but in a disturbing way.

Most ADHD students have a particularly hard time concentrating on things that don't interest them. Many are "burdened" by a bright mind that doesn't slow down. School is especially challenging due to its lock-step approach. These students often grow up into adults adept at inventing or at participating in creative new ventures where lots of simultaneous ideas lead to breakthroughs. When young, however, they usually find the "sit quietly, pay attention, raise your hand" mentality that most schools require especially difficult.

Because the autism spectrum ranges from intellectually gifted to severely disabled, it is impossible to offer a one-size-fits-all set of solutions. Many students with autism have sensory issues leading to hypersensitive reactions to touch, sound, or sight. The services of an occupational therapist can often help in this area. Most become extremely focused on something to the exclusion of everything else. Interrupting this focus can be unsettling and lead to anxiety or anger. Many children have difficulty correctly reading their immediate social circumstances, which often causes them to misinterpret other people's words or body language. It is therefore especially important to focus their attention on what we want instead of what we don't want. As well, it can be very helpful to articulate and validate their feelings. For example, "Your face is all crumpled up. If the noise bothers you, we can get your earplugs to make things quieter. Would you like us to do that?" It is not unusual for autistic students to have "meltdowns" when they are stressed, overwhelmed by sensory stimuli, or unable to express their needs. Without support, they can be easy targets for bullies.

Several strategies offered in Chapter 10 (on chronic misbehavior) are appropriate for students with these needs, such as integrating exercise throughout the day and teaching students better self-control through self-calming techniques. In addition, we offer many tips that can help these students achieve greater classroom success while minimizing the disruptions associated with their challenges. Whenever possible, these strategies should be offered as suggestions that leave room for the student to give input as well.

Classroom Management Strategies for Students with Excessive Energy

The following strategies are particularly appropriate for students with excessive energy, but other students may benefit from them as well.

• **Velcro.** Glue or tape a two-inch strip of Velcro underneath a student's desk or chair with the rough side accessible. Suggest to the student that when she feels the need to get out of her seat, she should first rub the Velcro. The stimulation of movement is usually all a student is seeking, and rubbing the Velcro often helps fill this need.

• **Fidget objects.** In addition to things like koosh balls, soft foam packing material, hair bands, and Silly Putty—all of which can be used to keep hands occupied—many websites specifically sell items for fidgeting silently (search online for "fidget items for classroom use"). Be sure to stay away from noisy items that usually create more problems than they solve.

• **Use of keyboards.** For students who have trouble writing things by hand, written assignments feel like torture. Such students are often more productive at a keyboard. Simply significantly reduce or remove handwriting requirements by giving them the opportunity to do their work on a computer, both at home and in class.

• **Swimming noodles.** Slice a swimming noodle into two or three sections (one noodle works for as many as three different students). Place a section at the feet of students who move their legs a lot, and allow them to roll it back and forth. Because the noodle is made of Styrofoam, it doesn't make any noise when rolled.

- **Industrial rubber bands.** These can be purchased at most home improvement stores. Place one around the legs of a student's chair or desk. The student can then quietly kick into the rubber band instead of the desk in front of him.

- **Music stands.** For students who prefer standing, place a few music stands around the perimeter of your classroom and let students do assignments while standing. This is a great strategy because the music stands are adjustable and have a hard, smooth surface that allows students to write while standing.

- **Controlled territory.** For elementary students, use masking tape to make a square (or some other familiar shape) around their desks. This becomes their personal "roaming space." Tell the student, "If you need to get up and move during a seated activity, this is your area. Let's see how well you can remember to stay inside it." Make the area big enough that the student has room to roam but small enough to limit distractions. The key to this strategy's success is not the amount of space provided as much as the boundary itself, which lends a sense of ownership and concrete structure.

- **Super-organizational structures.** Disorganization and disruption often go hand in hand. Many students who struggle continually lose and forget their things. Papers and notes are often disorganized and unmanageable. Notebooks are typically stuffed with papers from three or four different subjects. Super-organizers can help. Provide boxes (shoeboxes are perfect—let the students decorate the outsides), multicolored folders, and binders for each subject. When it's time to change classes or subjects, the student can place completed work in its own storage holder. Students often need considerable practice putting the right item in the correct location. Find a special place in the room for storing the organizers. It is also helpful to assign a well-organized student to coach a disorganized "buddy." The organized one can help make sure the disorganized peer has the proper materials and places papers in the correct file or folder.

- **Self-monitoring devices.** Many students with impulse-control issues have trouble monitoring their own behavior. One solution is to temporarily provide an external monitor. If a student frequently blurts out in class, it's OK to choose a reasonable number of blurts for a given time period. The number should be (1) within reach of the student's ability, (2) workable for you, and (3) reasonable for other students. Give the student markers for blurts to keep track of the number. Markers can include cards, pieces of tape, or a form of tokens (not candy or money). It is best for students to monitor the markers, but if they need help, take one away privately each time a student blurts. When the markers are gone, the student has no more blurts for that time period. Adjust the number of markers up or down if necessary. The long-term goal is to fade out the use of markers as the student improves monitoring his own behavior.

- **Seat placement.** Distractible students are not usually at their best in either rear or front seats. Rear seats are too far from the teacher, and front seats place their distractions center stage for all to see. The best placement is on the wings. You might say, "Amal, I'd like to change your seat because I think it will help you to concentrate better. Are you OK with that, or do you think there's an even better seat that will help you get your work done?"

- **Things to tap on.** Tapping pencils (or similar objects) drives us all crazy, but it's not the movement that does it—it's the noise. Tapping on sponges, piles of tissue paper, carpeting, or old mouse pads will do. Remove the noise, and would-be drummers can beat away without distracting others.

- **Time to wander.** Make movement a legitimate part of your students' day. When you notice restlessness creeping in, ask if they would like a drink or if they need to use the restroom. It is important for some students to be given time to work out of their seats during class. This can also be a good time to send a restless student on an errand. We know a teacher who asked a student to check all the water fountains to see how many of them needed repair.

- **Alternative desks.** We believe that it is just a matter of time before desks designed to accommodate movement become mainstream. Options including standing desks, pedal desks, and exercise-ball desks. Although cost concerns have limited the use of standing desks, preliminary reports from teachers whose students have used them suggest the targeted students display improved concentration and less need to wander (Kavilanz, 2017). The pedal desk is essentially a sized-down exercise bike with noiseless pedals designed to fit under a desk, offering students an opportunity to move and exercise during the day (Ogoe, 2015). An exercise-ball desk is essentially an exercise or stability ball placed within chair legs. Common sense would suggest that in addition to the classroom benefits, widespread use of these alternatives could also positively affect health issues such as obesity and diabetes.

Additional Strategies to Help Students with ADHD or Autism

The following strategies work well for students with ADHD or autism, and they can help other students who get easily overwhelmed.

• **Establish predictable routines, especially during transitions.** Many students with ADHD or autism do best when the environment is orderly and predictable. Try to avoid surprises. For example, it is usually best to avoid pop quizzes, unpredictable assignments, or unplanned activities. When the student is involved in an assignment or a project, avoid interruptions such as initiating spontaneous conversation. When interrupted, some students will completely ignore what was said and pretend it never happened, while others say the first thing that comes to mind, no matter how unrelated it might be. If transitions or surprises are on the horizon, warn the student in advance. Have the student sit near others who are high in empathy and caring to increase the likelihood of positive interactions.

• **Give specific assignments.** Be very specific in what you want. For example, say, "John, please do numbers 1, 2, and 3. Come and tell me when you have finished." You might also arrange some other signal (a raised hand, head resting on the desk, etc.) if you are concerned about the student contacting you too frequently.

• **Provide schedules.** Give students a planner or visual schedule so they know what is happening throughout the day. If you teach in a block schedule, write the times for each part of the class on the board. For example:

7:20–7:40 Poetry
7:40–8:00 Reading
8:00–8:20 Writing
8:20–8:40 Questions/begin homework

Now a student who struggles in any one of these areas knows, for example, she has to read for only 20 minutes and then the activity changes.

• **Develop interests through linking.** It is common for autistic students, in particular, to have an obsessive interest in a particular subject. To help them develop more flexible thinking, try to link their obsessive interest to another subject being studied in class. For example, if a student is obsessed with Christopher Columbus as an explorer but the class is studying space travel, try to have the student connect Columbus's mode of exploration on the seas to travel in space.

• **Shorten or modify assignments.** Because excessive focus and distractibility can be problems, shorten or alter assignments. If too much material appears on a single page, many students won't know where to focus and will become confused.

• **Teach social skills and nuances.** Understanding and using the nuances of language and social interaction are often major issues for autistic students. Be sure to provide direct instruction when words have multiple meanings. Idioms, analogies, and sarcasm can easily be misunderstood, so explain such language carefully. Without pushing too hard, model, teach, and practice nonverbal communication skills such as tone of voice, body language, various facial expressions, and personal space.

• **Use earphones to block sound.** When students appear unable to shut out extraneous sound, consider providing earphones.

Working with Difficult Parents

The following strategies will help you gain the support of challenging parents, defuse their anger, and turn them from adversary to ally. For a comprehensive look at this topic, we recommend *Turning Tough Parents into Strong Partners* (Mendler & Mendler, 2017).

Building and Sustaining Positive Relationships

Relationships require an ongoing effort if they are to be productive for everyone involved. Here are some ways to build—and maintain—positive relationships with parents.

• **Get on their side early.** Spend some time early in the school year figuring out who your challenging students are, and then contact their parents. Demonstrate interest by introducing yourself either in person or by phone. Tell them that you expect all of your students to be successful, and identify a few important guidelines that you expect your students to follow. Ask if they have any suggestions for things you can do to be a great teacher for their child. Quite simply, it is important to show that you care by enthusiastically expressing your desire to make it a successful year.

Caring goes a long way with parents and students. It is also important in other professions. Studying medical mistakes among primary care physicians, Levinson and her colleagues (1997) found no difference in the number and type of medical mistakes between those who had been sued and those who had not. However, the research showed that physicians who had never been sued spent 20 percent more time with their patients, used more humor, and showed more personal interest in patients than did those who had been sued. If primary care physicians can avoid malpractice lawsuits by spending a few more caring minutes with a patient, it is reasonable to assume that teachers, too, can avoid a lot of complaints from parents by conveying the human touch.

• **Form a team.** Difficult students find it advantageous to keep parents and teachers battling each other. Many parents think their child can do no wrong. Don't debate this view. Instead, emphasize how the child is hurting *himself* rather than how he is hurting you or the class. Invite parents to find things each of you can do to make the problem better. Parents are more willing to join with you to help their child than to help the school. Here are some examples of what you might say:

> "Let's think about how we can help him get here on time so he doesn't fall further behind in his work."

> "I probably do bother her more than she'd like because I'm concerned that she's letting herself down by giving up too quickly."

• **Ask, "What works at home?"** This question shows you respect what's happening at home. Many parents will tell you. Others will tell you they don't know, in which case you might ask if they can brainstorm with you some things to try in the classroom.

• **Make at least two phone calls home before problems occur.** Your first phone call to a parent should be to introduce yourself and your program. Before school begins, tell parents that you are looking forward to having their child in your class this year. Be clear and specific in letting them know what factors are most important for success in your classroom, such as study skills and good organization. You might ask them to describe their child in terms of study habits and organizational skills. Ask them to tell you a little bit about their child's past school experience, how she best learns, and what interests she has. The second phone call should be made sometime during the first two weeks. Offer a genuine compliment about something the student accomplished either academically or behaviorally.

• **Send complimentary notes home occasionally.** Sending a note to parents about an achievement or accomplishment pertaining to their child often generates much support. Everyone likes to hear good news about their child.

• **Call or text and leave a positive message.** To save time, simply call when you think nobody will be home or send a text to share a message of appreciation about something positive the student accomplished. Such a message can be especially use- ful after you have discussed a concern with a parent and notice improvement in the child. End with something like "Thanks for your help in influencing Krissy, because improvement is definitely happening—I just wanted to let you know."

• **Solicit information from parents.** To be successful, let parents know that you would like help in understanding their child. Specifically, ask them these questions:

"What are three things your child likes to do?"

"What are a few things that your child likes best about school?"

"What are two or three things you have noticed that help your child learn?"

"What are some things that I should know that could help me make school a successful place for your child?"

• **Ask to see pictures of the family.** This small gesture really has a big impact on how the parent will work with you. Most parents enjoy showing pictures of their children and appreciate your wanting to see them. Really look at the pictures, and make a sincere comment or two about them.

• **Share and explain your goals.** It is important for your discipline plan to be aligned with your instructional goals. For example, if your goals are to help each student be successful and to learn more about responsibility, then be prepared to explain to parents how a consequence or an intervention you chose is tied to furthering either or both of those goals for their child. Most parents are very supportive when they believe that you know their child and are choosing actions based on that knowledge.

• **Tell parents when they can contact you.** Many teachers feel stressed because they think they need to be on call for parents 24/7. Tell parents specifically when you are available; for example, "I am available by e-mail from 3 to 4 on Tuesday and Thursday and by phone from 3 to 4 on Wednesday." Setting things up this way also allows you to look good if you answer at 6 p.m. on a Sunday. In other words, it's good practice to underpromise and overdeliver.

Responding to Inappropriate Behavior from Parents

Despite your best efforts at fostering effective relationships with parents, they still may behave in inappropriate ways. Here are some strategies for addressing such flare-ups.

• **Allow the parent to let off some steam, within limits.** Then try to defuse the parent. Say something like "I know you're angry, Mrs. Jones, but swearing at me won't solve this problem."

• **Move around to refocus your nervous energy.** Moving will help you expel energy that might otherwise make you say something you'll regret.

• **Become softer, quieter, and slower.** If a parent turns up his volume, simply turn down yours.

• **Acknowledge the legitimacy of the complaint.** For example, you might say, "You're saying that your son thinks I'm unfair and boring. To better understand, what can you tell me about him that might help me get his interest and best effort?"

• **Call the parent before you send the child to the office.** The phone call can sound something like this: "Mr. Shaw, Andy has been having some trouble using proper language these last few days, and when I correct him, he has been getting angry with me. Before I get him involved with the office, I wanted to request your assistance. I wonder if you have any ideas about how to help him."

• **Separate the student and the parent.** If the student is present when the parent attacks inappropriately, ask the child to step out of the room for a moment, and then address the parent. Say something like this: "Ms. Richards, I know you're upset, but I don't want Jose to get the idea that it's OK to talk to adults in that tone of voice. Please do not talk to me like that." Immediately take charge by redirecting the conversation back on task. Later on, when all seems calm, you might invite the student back into the room.

• **Focus on the future.** Shift your and the parent's perspective away from the heat of the moment by saying something like, "Mrs. Lewis, what do you think we can do to help Steve avoid this kind of situation in the future?" or "Maybe you can talk with Steve tonight so he understands there are better choices he can make."

• **Be the good guy.** Let the parent know the consequence could have been worse. Say something like, "Ms. Hill, usually cheating means a zero and a discipline referral. But I'm going to go to bat for Tony. Because this is his first time, I think the zero is sufficient, and I'll advise the principal against any other consequences. I can't promise she'll see it this way, but I'll do my best."

• **Explain the difference between "fair" and "equal" treatment.** When parents complain about unfair treatment toward their child, you can say many things, but our favorite is this: "I can't talk specifics with you about other students because that is a private matter between myself, those students, and their parents. I can tell you that I try to do what I think is best for each child so he will benefit from his mistakes. If you'd like, I'll be happy to explain why I did [intervention] with your child." Then explain the difference between "fair" and "equal" (see pp. 89–91).

Interrupting the School-to-Prison Pipeline

"School-to-prison pipeline" is a term used to describe how some schools, largely in the inner city, prepare and even urge disenfranchised, primarily minority students in the direction of prison. Before we explain and offer solutions to this phenomenon, we should make clear that urban schools, like those in the suburbs, run the gamut from great to miserable. City schools offer many advantages, ranging from the cultural mix of the students to the incredible array of nearby institutions related to art, science, and technology. Many urban schools are alive with vitality, offering special programs unavailable to their suburban counterparts and a unique feeling of safety that protects their students from the uncertainties of the streets.

Yet many urban schools continue to struggle with serious issues, including a hardening of both teachers and students, decaying infrastructure, and scarce resources. One school we visited had a problem because many of the 3rd and 4th grade students had their sneakers stolen off their feet on the way to school. Too often, children need to walk to school on the same streets that rang out with gunshots the night before. Is it any wonder that many children might feel preoccupied with challenges other than academics?

One explanation of the school-to-prison pipeline describes it as

> . . . an epidemic that is plaguing schools across the nation. Far too often, students are suspended, expelled, or even arrested for minor offenses that leave visits to the principal's office a thing of the past. Statistics reflect that these policies disproportionately target students of color and those with a history of abuse, neglect, poverty, or learning disabilities. Students who are forced out of school for disruptive behavior are usually sent back to the origin of their angst and unhappiness—their home environments or their neighborhoods, which are filled with negative influence. Those who are forced out for smaller offenses become hardened, confused, embittered. Those who are unnecessarily forced out of school become stigmatized and fall behind in their studies; many eventually decide to drop out of school altogether, and many others commit crimes in their communities. (Amurao, 2013)

Suspensions and in-school arrests are often the first steps in the school-to-prison pipeline, and black and Latino students are disproportionately affected. Forty percent of all students suspended from school in the United States are black. Seventy percent of all in-school arrests are of black or Latino students (Amurao, 2013). New data show that the pipeline starts as early as preschool, where black preschool children were 3.6 times more likely to receive out-of-school suspensions than white children (Quinlan, 2016).

The data are troubling, but not surprising. For example, in Rochester, New York, home to two of the authors of this book, 51 percent of urban families have students living in poverty. Although poverty can be found in all settings, recent statistics show that the 100 largest metro areas accounted for 70 percent of all poor living in "extremely poor neighborhoods" (Kneebone & Holmes, 2016). A scarcity of nice low-income housing, jobs, and other resources contribute to the problem.

Throughout this book, we have described much of what works with difficult students in all schools. Especially relevant is the central tenet of disciplining students as a way to teach and influence better behavior rather than punishing them into better behavior. In this section, we highlight particularly helpful strategies for working with students who face major life issues that put them at high risk for entering the wretched school-to-prison pipeline.

• **Provide a supportive relationship.** Wang, Haertel, and Walberg (1997), among others, note that a teacher's concern, high expectations, and role modeling are key protective factors that mitigate against the likelihood of academic failure, particularly for students in difficult life circumstances. We have long advocated for a Big Brothers Big Sisters–type program right in school, where caring adults "adopt" one or two students (not currently in one's class) and provide mentoring and guidance on a regular basis. We were touched by an 8th grade class in a human relations course at an overcrowded school in a poor neighborhood in the Bronx. One student shared that her family had their extra money hidden under the living room rug. A classmate asked why this girl would reveal such confidential information. She replied, "In this class you are all my friends; I trust you." Just recently, one of the authors visited an inner-city elementary school that begins each day with a Boys Group for students with very high suspension rates. The group gives these students the opportunity to talk about issues, set daily goals, and learn effective nonviolent problem-solving skills. During the program's first six months, only one student had been suspended—once—and many students went on to become peer mediators. Chapter 5 offers many more ways to enhance relationships with difficult students.

Many schools in "tough" neighborhoods have police on staff. These officers should be looked to as a last resort for enforcement of difficult situations. They should teach classes in self-protection, be a friend to those who are being bullied, and do whatever they can to encourage trust and warm relations with students. They should never be seen as the enemy. Schools can build positive community relations with police. When called into classrooms, the role of police should be to enforce peace, not to humiliate or be tougher than necessary.

• **Respect social and cultural differences, but teach behaviors needed for success at school.** Many students live by a set of "street" norms that help them survive but are simultaneously harmful to their success at school. For example, physical fighting may be necessary to survive on the street, but it will always lead to major consequences at school. Students need to hear that our voices are consistent with their reality. When working to teach them alternatives, we must start by acknowledging their strengths. Many of the self-control strategies offered in Chapter 10 can be particularly helpful. Even if a student seems to have little or no interest in doing something different, perhaps we can succeed in getting him to wait until he is out of school that day and has a chance to cool off.

• **Welcome parents and interested adults to school.** Students with at least one parent who is strongly aware of what is going on at school and who communicates the value of education are far more likely to succeed than students who don't. We believe in a novel idea: schools should open their doors to all adults who did not graduate from high school and offer them opportunities to take classes. Adult education programs offered at school in which parents can work toward a GED or equivalent will begin getting parents to value education while their children are going to school. Make the signs at school welcoming. For example, "We Are Glad You Are Visiting Our School" should precede "We Ask That All Visitors Sign In at the Office Upon Entering." Two other strategies that are often well received are having a dedicated "parent" room that has coffee, fruit, and books on parenting, and offering scheduled seminars on how to help children learn at home.

• **Find helping hands both from outside and within the school.** Most urban schools lack the resources to hire more personnel to work with troubled youth. Fortunately, there are many cost-free solutions to this problem. For many years we have suggested inviting healthy senior citizens to become class grandmas and grandpas. Many seniors are lonely and bored and looking for a sense of purpose. Giving them the opportunity to help troubled youth in the classroom or, alternatively, having troubled youth befriend seniors at their homes, helps both groups in incredible ways.

Another typically unused resource is older students. There is no excuse for not giving a form of credit to older students who serve as tutors, role models, and counselors for younger, troubled students. Often older troubled students greatly benefit from the chance to do good (see the discussion of the altruism consequence on p. 91).

• **Provide help during and after school for students who need it.** Have tutors available to assist with assignments. Also, be sure students know they are welcome to stay after school to do their homework or get assistance. Students who are failing due to lack of effort should be required to stay after school for help until they get up to speed.

• **Make school the hub of community activity.** In many urban areas, school is the one place where all neighborhood students gather. We believe schools are therefore in a unique position to be the primary source from which people in the community receive the services they need. For example, it may be a lot easier to coordinate parent conferences at school if families' government assistance checks are awaiting them in an office inside the school after the conference. At the same time, if adult education classes were offered right after school, with babysitting or school activities simultaneously provided for children, it is likely more adults would attend. Too often in needy communities, many agencies and initiatives operate independently and lack coordination. Schools also should be the center of after-school activities for students so they have a safe place to do their homework or participate in recreational activities.

• **Enlist community leaders.** Contact as many community leaders as possible and ask to meet with them on a regular basis. Every city has both formal and informal groups and organizations that help the community. Some examples might be the local YMCA, the NAACP, places of worship, and cultural centers. Find out what their programs offer, what support they can give, and what support you can give them. Invite people involved in these organizations into your class to talk with students. Be sure to ask for any cultural insights that could be affecting student performance in the classroom so you can better understand subtle changes that might make a difference.

• **Capitalize on the resources in the city.** Cities offer a variety of resources that cannot be matched elsewhere. The arts, business and industry, parks, museums, and a multitude of people are all within reach for the creative inner-city teacher. Working independently or with a group of other teachers, use the city itself as a teaching laboratory for experiences related to your content area. Visit businesses, hospitals, the police station, museums, libraries, planetariums, historical landmarks, and other spots that are sometimes taken for granted. Use the extensive cultural diversity that exists in most cities to explore the richness each culture brings through its customs, values, and historic contributions. Arrange trips to the nearest rural areas whenever possible (some city children never see a live cow or a field of food crops until they are adults). Bring city resources into your school if you cannot take students out. One school made an arrangement with a local college to let its architectural students transform a hallway into an arboretum and another hallway into a library, and to build time-out areas in five classrooms.

• **Invite new dreams without encouraging the "unrealistic."** Urban students from impoverished areas often tell us they want to be professional football or basketball players. Many others want to be the next great rapper. Although teachers should never attempt to kill a student's dreams, it is our responsibility to point out viable alternatives should the lofty original goal not be met. For example, if by 11th grade a student has not yet made the varsity team, the probability of making the NBA is extremely remote. The more options troubled students have in areas that influence their life choices, the more hope they have for success. A student might not make it to the NBA but could become a physical education teacher and be around sports all the time. Students could also aspire to becoming a coach or a referee, making a nice living being in the sport they love. Students who want to be entertainment stars can be shown that working in music production studios might be an option as well.

Another point to consider is the belief among some people that academics are becoming less important in the technical world of today. Many high-tech companies aren't looking for traditional college graduates as much as those with technical skills. Many students could be diverted from the school-to-prison pipeline if we placed more emphasis on training in skilled trades and technical occupations that can lead to high-paying jobs rather than traditional academic classes that students too often view as irrelevant.

* * * * * * *

To conclude this chapter, we offer the following anonymous poem that you can copy, blow up, and post in your classrooms:

The Bottom Line
Face it.
Nobody owes you a living.
What you achieve or fail to achieve in your lifetime
is directly related to what you do
or fail to do.
No one chooses his parents or childhood,
but you can choose your own direction.
Everyone has problems and obstacles to overcome,
but that too is relative to each individual.

Nothing is carved in stone.
You can change anything in your life
if you want to badly enough.
Excuses are for losers.
Those who take responsibility for their actions
are the real winners in life.

Winners meet life's challenges head-on,
knowing there are no guarantees,
and give it all they've got.
It's never too late or too early to begin.
Time plays no favorites
and will pass whether you act or not.

Take control of your life.
Dare to dream and take risks.
If you aren't willing to work for your goals,
don't expect others to.

Believe in yourself!

—Anonymous

12

Guide for Administrators

Effective administrators set goals, evaluate performance, monitor teachers and students, and model appropriate ways to behave and act. Discipline starts for the administrator by creating an atmosphere that encourages free and open discussion with teachers, without fear of censure. Teachers worry that they will be considered weak or incompetent if they admit to problems with student behavior. When we ask groups of teachers, "Raise your hand if you have discipline problems," very few hands go up. When we ask the same group, "Raise your hand if you know another teacher dealing with behavior problems," just about every hand is raised.

The Discipline with Dignity approach is flexible enough to fit the needs and issues of all schools and teachers. In the same way administrators suggest teachers focus on student strengths, we recommend they help teachers identify unique individual strengths they each have in relation to discipline and content instruction. Talk individually to teachers about what they are passionate about and help them unleash it within their individual teaching style. Some are great lecturers. Others are good at facilitating group work. Encourage teachers to focus on those qualities while improving other areas that might make them even better. Improvement in managing a classroom can be made by building on these teacher strengths. Some teachers may not see how the degree of enthusiasm they have for what they teach can have a powerful effect on student behavior. Other teachers may feel limited by their interpretation of the curriculum or your expectations, believing that either prevents them from being the teacher they want to be.

To ensure that teachers receive the support they want and expect, ask each to discuss plans for preventing discipline problems from occurring. Ask to see their social contract (see Chapter 6) and discuss it with them. Be sure the rules and consequences specified in the social contract are compatible with the school's mission and values. Involve teachers in the development of schoolwide rules and consequences. Let them know what you consider to be valid reasons (e.g., issues of safety, inability to teach, need for an occasional time-out) and less valid reasons (everything else) to involve you in classroom discipline issues.

Be sure to provide adequate inservice training, especially on how to quickly de-escalate most situations. Discuss possible cultural differences and how those can affect both verbal and nonverbal communication. Invite teachers to develop classroom discipline methods according to four criteria:

- Does it work?
- Does it preserve dignity, or does it humiliate?
- Does it teach responsibility, or does it rely on obedience?
- How does it affect motivation to learn?

Reflect Vision in the School Discipline Plan

School faculties represent a wide range of feelings, beliefs, and attitudes pertaining to discipline. Some support many rules and harsh consequences. Others are more lenient and emphasize students solving their own problems. As the school leader, your vision is most influential. Effective school discipline requires a common vision focused primarily on what is best for students. Be sure to clearly articulate yours. Challenge teachers and encourage them to challenge each other to articulate beliefs and practices. Push them to improve while respectfully asking how their beliefs and practices are in the best interest of students. A key to a school's success is that staff members feel respected for their thoughts and ideas while also understanding that they will be expected to enforce some rules—even those they disagree with. Explain to your staff that saying, "I don't agree with this rule, but I have to enforce it" suggests weakness and is almost an invitation for students to break rules. It's better to say, "This is the rule of the school, and because I choose to work here, I choose to enforce that rule. We are a community here."

To help focus discussion, begin with the list of in-school causes of misbehavior described in Chapter 2. Create groups or committees dedicated to each cause. The committees can develop a specific plan to address each area. The standard for all policies and practices must be to do what is best for students.

A group in a suburban middle school gave students control by creating a student committee that included "disruptors" and "troublemakers" to help set school policy related to rules and consequences. These types of committees are most beneficial when they develop a specific plan for action. The plan should state what needs to be implemented, who will do it, when it will be completed, and how it will be evaluated. Each member of the school community (teachers, parents, administrators, students, nurses, bus drivers, other staff) must know clearly what his or her responsibilities include.

School leaders should help faculty keep in perspective the relatively *minor* role that rules and consequences play in overall discipline. Although a social contract is the backbone of the formal discipline process, on its own it does not address the causes of discipline problems. For example, many problems are the result of poor student motivation, not discipline. Provide training or coaching in developing students' motivation skills and improved instructional techniques for those teachers who need it (see Chapter 8). The more students are motivated, the fewer discipline problems will exist.

Emphasize *attitude* and *effort*. Teach and lead the staff to know that these two words are the most important words to emphasize in the effort to achieve success in the classroom. The attitude teachers and students take and the effort they put in are what matter most. Explore with staff how to use grades and other methods of evaluation to reflect effort at least as much as achievement. They will need support from the school leader to create a system that emphasizes competition with oneself based primarily on effort and progress rather than comparison. If teacher evaluation is at least partially based on achievement, look for ways to compare progress made from the beginning to the end of the school year rather than achievement of an arbitrary standard set by outsiders. Improvement is the best single measure of academic success because it is the only measure that students can control.

Encourage teachers to use grade-level and subject-area meetings to create lessons that connect content to student interests as often as possible. Remind teachers regularly that a plan for discipline prevention involves addressing the needs for attention, connection, identity, competence, control, and fun.

Emphasize the Importance of Relationship Building

Much of this book is about sharing methods that work, preserve dignity, emphasize responsibility, and do not adversely affect motivation to learn. The administrators set the tone by having clear and consistent rules and core values and by holding staff accountable. Be in the halls, cafeteria, and bus loop when students arrive and leave. Occasionally ride the bus home with students. Be willing to fill in for a teacher and have direct, positive interactions with students inside the classroom.

Difficult students frequently seek a leader. Give teachers ideas for building relationships with students, and set aside faculty time for them to share ideas with one another. Explain why relationships are so important. If teachers do not know student interests, it will be impossible for them to design a lesson supporting individual needs. Teach them to spend time outside class getting to know their students. Go to games, recitals, and events—and encourage teachers to do the same. Do not allow excuses. If teachers say, "I have my own children all afternoon so I can't go to an event," encourage them to take their kids along. When teachers are seen at school-promoted events, students notice and are likely to spend less time off task. Ask questions about home lives, and never be afraid to share details about yours.

A principal we know in Illinois asks teachers to create an "All About Me" poster board for their room with pictures of their family, interests, friends, and activities. Teachers are required to spend two weeks building relationships before teaching any content. They share their hopes, dreams, and core values with their students.

Nurture staff as you want them to nurture students. Take care of staff by having fun. Laugh with them. Occasionally cancel a staff meeting at the last minute, but then invite everyone to join you for pizza. Help teachers identify causes of stress and search for strategies to fix the situation without taking on the responsibility of rescuing them. Avoid stress by putting teachers in positions where they are likely to succeed. Teachers do better when teaching to their strengths. Notice the teachers who stay late with certain students. Privately and genuinely show how much you appreciate them. Remember special events like birthdays. We know an administrator who brings in a chair masseuse for the second half of inservice days. Staff get 15-minute massages of head, neck, and shoulders in the school lobby.

Deal with Referrals in Productive Ways

Explain to staff members that every time they send a student to the office, they disempower themselves. They send students the message "I can't handle you on my own. I need help." Although this is the not the message the teacher is trying to send, it is what students often receive, and it is a dangerous message to communicate to tough kids. The message should be "Get used to me because it is almost impossible to get removed from my class." Role-play various scenarios that lead to referrals while demonstrating other ways to handle misbehavior in the classroom.

Recognize that a teacher referral is usually an expression of frustration, a lack of knowledge, or an unwillingness to see misbehavior as a problem primarily requiring their involvement to solve. Sometimes teachers simply need a deserved break to prevent an escalation of emotions. Other times they cannot or do not want to deal with the student. Be a good listener when receiving unwarranted referrals. Remember, although some referrals may seem minor compared with everything else administrators are focused on at any given time, to that teacher on that day in that moment, it is important.

Some teachers want administrators to be "tough" when students are referred. Your message to teachers should be that once a teacher gives up the opportunity to problem-solve with the student, it is at the discretion of the administrator as to how the referral will be handled. Let staff know that your goal is achieving improved behavior with interventions that are compatible with school values, not "toughness."

Help the student create a plan for behaving upon returning to class. Assure staff that you will do your best to send back a better behaved student, but remind them that rarely can you do it alone. Students with chronic behavior problems often revisit old behaviors several times while acquiring new behaviors. You will almost always need the teacher's assistance, which might mean expecting the teacher to respond differently to the student. When appropriate, offer to facilitate a positive student confrontation between the teacher and student (pp. 149–151).

Use this book for book-study groups or pick out examples of how to respond differently to difficult situations and have teachers practice. Remind them that because we have limited control over the many out-of-school causes of misbehavior, to get improved behavior we all need to work extra-hard to make school a positive experience for disconnected students.

After sending a student back to class, seek feedback about how things went for the remainder of class, and explore other options going forward if necessary. If possible, walk students back to class so the teacher knows you spent time with them. Your presence often prevents "saving face" behaviors after the student returns. When a student is sent to the office, allow at least 15 minutes before sending her back. Many teachers send students to the office for temporary relief and really appreciate some time apart.

Defusing power struggles is not easy. Emotions run high, and the teacher might not know how or when to back off. Let teachers know early in the school year that your involvement is necessary in situations that involve physical violence and when things are so bad they literally cannot teach. Encourage staff to send students to one another when they are at their wit's end from irritating behaviors and in need of some space.

The best administrators are always teachers first. Help students and teachers improve student interactions by encouraging teachers to handle, dissect, and create a plan to facilitate and solve their own problems. If possible, take time to review and ask questions about the referral with the teacher before meeting with the student or parent. Use open-ended questions, and guide teachers to think about various options and consequences when handling each student. In some cases, these actions may eliminate the discipline referral altogether. Finally, remind teachers that 10 percent of students are referred 90 percent of the time, and that 10 percent of teachers do 90 percent of the referring. The less a teacher uses the referral system, the more likely you are to take seriously that teacher's problem with a student.

Listen to Ideas

Teachers appreciate your being available at specific times to hear concerns and ideas. Listen respectfully to all ideas, and stay open-minded to well-conceived teacher alternatives to district policies, procedures, or zero-tolerance initiatives. If teachers are unhappy with a discipline policy or procedure they are expected to enforce, they should be welcome to propose an alternative. An administrator we know said this to her staff at her first faculty meeting:

> This is our country. We all have a say. Please keep in mind that each of us runs a state, but I have to oversee all of it. Once in a while your state might be asked to do something for the good of the country that you may not understand at first. If that happens, you are welcome to question a decision, and I will do my best to explain. If you think you have a better way, I will certainly listen, but please try to keep in mind that I have to consider how a decision that affects you might affect everyone else. For example, I might decide to assign a few more citizens to your state because I think putting them there would be better than putting them somewhere else. You might not be happy about that because it could upset the balance you have, but ultimately

I have to consider what is best for all our citizens. Faculty meetings are our time to get together and discuss matters that affect us all. In addition, I will do my very best to give notice in advance to any state about a decision that I think will directly affect you more than others. If you have a specific complaint along with a solution, please make an appointment. I am available from 6 a.m. until 7 a.m. on Monday and Wednesday mornings.

This administrator purposely sets aside times that are inopportune for many, to differentiate staff who are truly committed from those who just like to complain. She also leaves open the possibility of a different individual meeting time if it is impossible for a person to make it.

We believe it is usually best for teachers to decide what intervention is best for each classroom situation. Encourage them to think outside the box when a policy isn't working with a student or class. Let them know you appreciate new ideas. If you are uncertain about the likely effectiveness of a proposed alternative, agree to accept it for a trial period unless it seems harmful or unreasonable. Remember to emphasize how "fair" does not always mean "equal." Doing so leads to less worry about allowing deviations from school policy when that policy is not working. It also frees decision makers to do what they think is best for each student or class without making comparisons. For example, if the decision to assign a few students to a particular teacher makes her class disproportionately larger than those of colleagues, explain the reasoning by highlighting her strengths instead of possible limitations. When a teacher makes a comparative complaint—such as "Why does he have 24 students and I have 28?"—respond with something like this: "Thanks for taking a few more. Fortunately for the students, your talent makes me think you can have more success with them. I cannot discuss other teachers, but I promise to support you in whatever ways may be necessary to help you make this situation work. I will do my best to make it up to you in other ways." This approach reduces complaints and gossip among faculty and staff. Although it is always appropriate to treat everyone with respect and dignity, fairness with staff members means helping each one become as successful with students as possible.

Model the Behavior You Want to See

Lead and manage teachers and students the same way you want teachers to address uncooperative students. If they blame, complain, or use sarcasm, show them how to stay personally connected to students without taking personally what they do and say (see p. 136 in Chapter 9). You can do this during staff meetings. For example, if you are blamed for being "unsupportive," you can say, "So as you see it, there are other things I can do with your difficult students that might help make things work better for your class. Let's get together after the meeting, when I can really hear you out." It is hard for teachers to not take offensive behavior personally. Teach staff how to stand up to inappropriate behavior without allowing anger and frustration to take over. Explain how to become a "second-to-last-word person." Emphasize walking away and other informal methods as the best ways to handle inappropriate behavior in the moment.

Even teachers with lots of experience and good reputations worry about asking for help with discipline. They prefer to hide problems for fear of receiving a poor evaluation. Let them know you understand the stress it causes to pretend everything is fine when it is not. Assure them you would rather know they are struggling so you can take steps to improve the situation. Share the plan with the teacher before observing. Your goal is always to improve discipline and not to collect information for a formal evaluation. Help teachers learn to work through student discipline problems. In public (with other staff, students, parents), do your best to "have their back" (e.g., "I'm pretty sure it was Ms. Smith's intent to correct your daughter from continuing to make the same mistake, not to embarrass her"). Privately tell the truth. If the teacher is pouring gasoline on a tiny fire, tell him. Here's an example: "I don't enjoy saying this, but you [teacher] are contributing to the problem. Every time you publicly reprimand her, she blows up. Talk to her privately. Stop calling her out in front of her friends. Please change the way you approach her; while she might not become a model student, I know you'll have more success with her."

Support Staff by Observing Some Key Points

Teachers need a lot of support when working with chronically disruptive students. To help them, keep these points in mind:

• **Continue to involve the parents of chronically misbehaving students.** Remind teachers periodically that the likelihood of getting much greater parent support is higher when they occasionally call or text to share good news. Tell them to not be afraid to call parents at home and at work when need be (it's OK to ask parents for their work schedules). Remind them to try not to interrupt. If teachers need an uncooperative parent to come to school, intercede when there is a problem, and if necessary, use whatever leverage you have. If parents claim they cannot leave work, tell them you are sure their child is sorry for the inconvenience and that she will be waiting in the hall in 20 minutes for pickup. Keep parents of disruptive students informed of their children's progress.

• **Become an effective mediator** in the positive student confrontation method (p. 149), drawing upon your knowledge of both the student and the teacher. Be sure to explain the purpose and the process to both, but especially to the teacher, before proceeding. It might be helpful to list the steps in a convenient place and refer to them if needed.

• **Appeal directly to the families or community to assist with resolution.** The family intervention process (p. 151) can be an effective way to get key family members and educators to collaborate with challenging students by creating a plan for improved behavior. If problems involving several children in a classroom might have racial or gang overtones, involving the police and social agencies can often be helpful. Communities can also help. We know an inner-city school district that created a "violence-free zone" with a local social organization. They trained conflict mediators and troubleshooters to head off trouble before it happened by closely monitoring students known to be challenging. Suspensions dramatically decreased.

- **Encourage teachers to try new approaches.** Teachers have little to lose when trying unconventional strategies, but they often fear administrative disapproval or lack of support. Let them know you will support most of their plans that are nonpunitive. Ask them to share ideas with you in advance.

- **Remember that working with difficult students is frustrating!** Understand that when a teacher is calling a student names, demanding you act swiftly, or in some other way behaving "unprofessionally," this is the time for support, not debate. Help teachers feel less frustrated by sharing information concerning the student *and* by being a good listener who can express empathy.

- **Put teachers in a position to succeed.** Teachers do better with difficult students when teaching within their strengths. Avoid having one teacher be responsible for teaching all subjects to a self-contained class. Instead, allow a teacher who prefers English and math to teach those two subjects to two classes while another teaches social studies and science.

School administrators are not the only ones blamed for school problems, but they are usually the first target and often are on the receiving end of most complaints. They are held accountable by the office of the superintendent as well as by parents, students, and teachers. Administrators are especially vulnerable if they rose from the ranks of the faculty in the same school. To be most effective, they need to be friendly to everyone and friends to no one. In reality, administrators do have faculty friends, but the claim of favoritism lurks around every corner.

The remedy for all this pressure is within the pages of this book. Our most important strategy is to develop school values. Regardless of complaints, dissatisfaction, or blame, use the values to guide every decision you make. You might not end the pressure, but you will always know you are heading in the right direction.

Conclusion

We can do many things quickly and easily, like microwaving food or using a remote to turn on the TV. Helping children to nurture and grow is not one of them. It takes time and is rarely easy. It's a lot faster to kick a student out of class than it is to resolve a conflict or teach a student how to handle challenges more appropriately. Too many of our troubled students come to us without the foundational skills they will need to be successful: cooperating, sharing, solving problems peacefully, thinking before acting.

The following poem appeared in the first edition of this book, and it provided inspiration to answer the questions it posed:

Whose school is this, anyway?
Is it the principal's?
Is it the teachers'?
Is it the smart kids'?
Is it the shy kids'?
Is it the pushy kids'?
Is it the popular kids'?
Is it each kid's equally?
Is it the kids', the principal's, and the teachers' equally?
Who decides what goes on in here?

Who does it go on for?

Does it go on for the kids who go to college?

Does it go on for the kids who go to work?

Does it go on for the kids who have nowhere to go?

Does it go on for all kids equally?

Does it go on for the teachers?

Does in go on for the principal?

Does it go on for the teachers, the kids, and the principal equally?

Who tells whom what to do?

Who makes the rules?

Who are the rules for?

Who must follow the rules?

Who must see that the rules are followed?

Whose school is this, anyway?

We believe these two pillars of Discipline with Dignity will never change:

1.   School is for all children, including those who don't want to be there and those who haven't yet figured out how to be.

2.   You can help an educator without helping children, but when you help children, everyone benefits.

Over the years of our experience with Discipline with Dignity, we have been told by rabbis that our ideas come right from the Torah, by priests and ministers that it springs from Christianity, by Muslims that it is compatible with the Koran, by Native American educators that it comes right out of their culture. Although it is very satisfying to hear people of different religions and cultures express an important connection for them, it has been extremely gratifying to have heard countless educators tell us not only how helpful our strategies have been with their students, but also how the Discipline with Dignity approach has changed their lives for the better. Most have shared how it has provided a time-tested, solid structure for effective behavior management that relies primarily on dignity and respect rather than punishment, threat, tickets, and rewards. Many have especially appreciated the tools it provides to influence real change among students who make themselves hard to like without resorting to rancor and ill will. We hope this new edition, with its updated framework and many practical methods, continues that tradition.

Appendix:
Questions and Answers

Over the last 10 years we have been asked many questions about Discipline with Dignity. Here are our answers to those asked most frequently.

Because success is important in promoting positive behavior but mistakes and failures are a natural part of learning, how do I convince students to realize this and not give up when things get difficult?

Allen: Take action. Mistakes are reminders that none of us are perfect and that it takes courage and persistence to try to get better at anything worthwhile. Consider having a "3 Rs" policy to encourage improvement. Let students know that while you expect their best effort on all assignments and tests, they can "redo, retake or revise" an assignment or test until you or they are satisfied that their performance is about as good as it can be for now. Because some students may purposely put off doing their best initially, a small deduction in their grade (e.g., 5 points subtracted for each subsequent *R*) can be included. Such a policy makes it impossible for any students to fail unless they quit, especially if at least a portion of each student's grade is based on showing steady improvement.

Children are always told that it is OK to make mistakes because that is how they learn. Yet we often reward only the best answers or performances. If we want students to really believe that we are encouraging them to learn from their mistakes, then we need to actually point out the benefits when we see them. Get in the habit of explaining what mistakes teach. Here is a suggested sequence for explanation:

1. You [student] show a good understanding of [identify a strength in the work that showed the kind of thinking you were looking for].

2. Your mistake is a good reminder to [explain or give new information that promotes better understanding].

3. To be sure you now better understand, I'd like you to do a few more for practice [give specific practice problems].

Offer congratulations when the student shows improvement (e.g., "Way to go!").

Rick: Focus on effort. Not all students can achieve at the same level, but all students can try. When students try their best, they achieve their best. Honor improvement, seeking or giving help to others. Encourage extra assignments and freely chosen projects. No one in your class should ever fail, regardless of their scores, if they try. Likewise, no one should get the highest grades without demonstrating effort.

Brian: Make sure students succeed. With success comes confidence, which breeds more success. This is a cycle that many students have never felt. When kids begin swimming, they start in the shallow end with floaties because success is critical to gain confidence. Allow notes and retakes. Reward mistakes. Say, "The mistake you made is fantastic. I am sure many others made it, too. Do you mind me sharing with the class?" Your goal is to create an environment where failure is simply on the path to success.

What do you do with an entire class of disrupters?

Allen: Focus much more on behavior than academics for at least the first two weeks of the school year, if necessary. Start on day one by telling, showing, and practicing procedures that are necessary to experience success in class. How do you expect students to enter the classroom, and what should they do when they arrive? How should they seek permission, ask a question, get help? If and when they feel frustrated, angry, or upset, what are acceptable and unacceptable ways to express those emotions? Present options to them, like telling you after class and sending you a note. Anticipate and counteract restlessness and hyperactivity by building movement into lessons when possible and permitting some students to stand while working (see Chapter 11). Go beyond whatever consequences there may be for not being prepared by letting students know how they can successfully participate despite their forgetfulness. Explain and have them practice how to respectfully disagree. Reinforce appropriate behavior by pointing it out ("I really appreciate how Matthew asked Sabrina if it was OK to share the crayons she was using rather than grabbing them").

Confront inappropriate behavior simply, firmly, and directly but with dignity (e.g., "We don't say that here"; "That was disrespectful. You're better than that"). Meet with those students later on to reinforce, teach, and, if necessary, practice a better way of expressing their thoughts and feelings. In essence, anticipate problems that are most likely to trigger a loss of self-control, such as disagreements with other students, put-downs, a poor grade, boredom, and unfair treatment by the teacher. Then identify and practice whatever rules and procedures may be necessary to prevent problems from occurring or escalating. Many students with self-control problems benefit from having achievable daily goals. Ask them two questions at the beginning of class: "What are at least two things you need to keep in mind as we start the day [class]? What do you need from me to achieve those goals?" Finally, notice when the problem is absent or less obvious at school, and point out that students already have what it takes. Here's an example: "Connor, it was really great to see how you kept your cool when the hall monitor not-so-politely told you and your buddies to move along. How'd you make that happen? Did you take a few deep breaths, tell yourself to chill out, or do something else?"

Rick: Most students with poor self-control lack the ability to monitor their own behavior. Teach them self-monitoring devices as a way to gain self-control. For example, with the student's knowledge, keep a record of how many times he does a specific troublesome behavior during a specific time period each day for a week. At the end of the week, in a private conversation, ask him to guess how many times he did the behavior. Then show him how his guess compares with your record. The farther apart the numbers are, the less aware the student is of what he is doing. At first, the goal is not to reduce the number of incidents but to improve his awareness of his behavior. If his guess is more accurate, you can work on reduction. Do not use rewards or punishments in any way during this process. Doing so will change the focus and goal of the exercise, rendering it fruitless as a means to a long-term solution.

Brian: The first step is realizing the entire class is not disruptive. Every group has a leader. Figure out which students get the others off track. Focus on them. Build relationships with these leaders. Find them when you are not required to teach them. Walk around the school with them for 10 minutes and talk about anything but school. Tell them about your struggles and success in life. Ask questions and follow-up questions. Really get to know them. Remember, we need these few students more than they need us. They will help control the others.

My school has students move in and out during the school year. The arrival of one difficult student can change the chemistry of the class. How do I minimize disruption when this happens?

Allen: The arrival and departure of students during the school year can create challenges for classroom cohesion, so have procedures in place to help new students transition. Pair new students with "mentor" students who have the responsibility of welcoming newcomers by doing such things as touring the school together, eating lunch together, and sharing important classroom rules and procedures. Interestingly, many difficult students act very responsibly when given this role. As well, you can quickly determine new students' talents, needs, and preferences by interviewing them or asking them to complete an interest inventory.

Good classroom chemistry happens when kids believe in themselves and support and root for each other. Early on, celebrate the success of a new student by rewarding the group. For example, "Carlos's special effort this morning gets us all five extra minutes of recess. Enjoy." Get students involved in creating and modifying classroom rules. When new students arrive, ask if there were any other rules in their last school they found helpful. If a difficult student has trouble behaving, you might meet separately with one or more of your stronger students and ask them to reach out to that student. For example, "Hey guys, it seems that Matt is struggling to figure things out. Sometimes kids do things that bother others because they don't know any other way to feel special. Because you guys seem to be widely respected, I think if you reach out to him, his behavior might improve, and that would be good for everyone. Some ways I can think of are [name the ways]. What are some of your ideas?"

Students who tend to upset classroom balance usually have unmet basic needs for connection, competence, or control—or all three. Unless appropriate classroom channels are available, these students often take a disproportionate share of classroom time by calling attention to themselves and bothering others. You can often minimize the likelihood of disruption by welcoming them, involving them, and setting them up for success.

Perhaps most important is to let your students know that their daily success is your most important goal, and to define that success as all students getting better, wiser, or more able each day than they were the day before. You might have them keep a daily improvement journal, which reinforces the idea that learning is ongoing. If possible, try to minimize academic competition by making at least a significant portion of each student's grade dependent on improvement. Give properly challenging assignments that are difficult to fail. For example, you can encourage a discouraged student who is trying to hide inadequacy by refusing to work if you privately say something such as this: "I'd like to see you do all six of these problems, but focus your attention on number two because I'm going to call on you for the answer, and I want you to feel confident. Let's look at it together."

Rick: Along with excitement about a new beginning, new students may feel sad about losing old friends and familiar places, and perhaps favorite things to do. They also come with some fear of being disliked by their new peers. Try asking for five volunteers to be a new student's "friend" on each of her first five days. The new friend can introduce the new student to other students, be sure she doesn't eat alone, and offer to help with schoolwork. Be sure to place the student with new partners and groups as part of the instructional process.

Remember, too, that students who are leaving your school have similar feelings about the new school they will be attending. Just before a student leaves, divide the class into small groups. Ask each group to make a proclamation of good wishes for the student's future.

Brian: Privately ask new students what they are good at and enjoy. Introduce them to others with the same interests. Do everything to make them feel comfortable. Let them know that if they feel lost after watching you teach on the first day, they need not worry. Tell them it's rare for a new teacher to pick up exactly where a previous teacher left off, and that after class the two of you can figure out where the student is in terms of learning content. Be sure new students have a place and people to sit with at lunch, on the bus, and in any other less supervised area in school. As always, focus on relationships first.

My 5th grade students struggle with quieting down. I frequently shout at them, but I hate shouting. What do you recommend?

Rick: When I was a new teacher, I would stand in front of the class and say nothing until the students came to order. This tactic worked for about five days. After that, I could have stood there for a week, and the students wouldn't have noticed or cared. Every technique has a limited shelf life. The best solution is to find 10 or 12 tactics to use and rotate them every week or two, depending on your students' age. To create your list, ask your colleagues for suggestions, go online, and, of course, ask your students. Here are a few to get you started:

• Choose three to four "shushers," rotated weekly, to help you shush the class down when you need things to be quiet. Form small groups and let each group choose a new shusher each week. When you ask, it's the shushers' job to quiet their group.

• Have your students make a list of their favorite songs. Play one every time you need it quiet. Be sure to tell your students that when they hear the song, it's time for quiet.

• Raise your hand and ask students to raise theirs and stop talking when they see you.

• Write a somewhat silly question on the board. Tell students they can write down an answer to the question after things have quieted down. Once the class is ready to work, let students read their answers before the lesson continues.

Brian: Instead of shouting, listen! What are your students talking about? Can you take what they are talking about and turn it into a lesson? Are some students louder than others? If so, work harder to build relationships so they want to listen. Before things get excessively noisy, tell a disruptive student, "I am counting on you to help me get the others quiet. Can I count on you? Can I trust you?" Look for leadership roles for the noisiest students. Set aside specific times for kids to be noisy. Then say, "Guys, right now is not that time. But I promise: give me 20 minutes of work and I will give you 5 minutes of noisy time."

Allen: If the noisiness occurs during a transition period—for example, between an energizing group activity and a teacher-led lesson—try using strategies like lights on-off, hand raising, and counting to signal the transition. In addition, for group activities, each group can have a designated student "quieter" whose primary responsibility is to keep track of how much time remains. When two minutes remain, use an auditory signal, such as chimes or a bell, to alert the class that the activity will soon end. The "quieter" uses the final two minutes to have the group wrap up. Kids who have the most trouble quieting down often make the best quieters. When the group time is down to the last 20 seconds, say, "Down to 20," and count aloud backward until you reach 1.

If the issue is too much socializing, consider giving students a few minutes of class time to socialize. For example, "I know this is math, and that's where we need to spend most of our time. But I know you guys like to know what's going on in each other's lives, so you get three minutes to socialize at the beginning or end of class. Your choice. That may or may not be enough time, but it's all the time there'll be." Then take a vote or, if you prefer, alternate social time between the beginning and end of class. Another option is to occasionally and unexpectedly show appreciation by giving students time to socialize; for example, "You guys have been great today. Take these next few minutes to let your mind relax, either by yourself or with a friend."

What is the difference between motivation and manipulation, and why does it matter?

Rick: The difference between manipulation and motivation matters a lot, not only for academic involvement but also for behavior. The goals of both are similar, and that's what makes them confusing. However, they are opposites. Manipulation gets students to work for reasons other than learning. Motivation means a desire to do something—such as learn. Teachers manipulate and motivate to get students to do their work and make good behavioral choices. Many teachers don't care which method is used as long as their desired goals are achieved. I've heard teachers say, "I got that student to do his homework. Does it really matter how?"

But students feel very differently when they do something because they have to or because they want to. As we have said throughout this book, threats, punishments, and rewards are tools of manipulation; from the student's point of view, learning or making a good behavioral choice is secondary to either getting what he wants or avoiding having something bad happen to him. Students who are being manipulated tend to do whatever is necessary, but little, if anything, more. We call students like these "finishers" because their goal is to bring an end to the situation. By contrast, motivation relies on pride, interest in improving, the desire to dig deeper academically, and caring about how behavior might affect others. So although both manipulation and motivation may produce results, those results are not of the same quality.

Brian: Motivation is choosing to do something because we intrinsically see its benefit and value. Manipulation is doing something because someone convinces us to do so by hiding his or her true intentions.

Allen: The main difference is intent. Manipulating is when you persuade people that you can do something for their benefit when it actually is for yours. Bernie Madoff manipulated investors into believing that he could make money for them. He intentionally lied by using his status, knowledge, and friendships to enrich himself at the expense of others. Motivation is influencing someone to do something for the benefit of that individual. You may benefit as a result, but there is no deception involved. Manipulation works only until the victim realizes he's been "had."

I'm a new teacher. Everyone says I should be mean and make the students afraid before I can lighten up. Should I start tough?

Rick: Neil Postman once wrote that "kids have built-in crap detectors." He meant that students can tell when a teacher is being dishonest with them. If you try to be different than you are by acting tough, your students will figure out the illusion fairly quickly and test you to see how far you will go. Perhaps even worse is that you won't like yourself very much in your new role.

I fully agree with the idea of showing strength as long as the effort is genuine. Using the tools of proximity, eye contact, and privacy (see Chapter 7) shows more strength than a phony portrayal of toughness. Real toughness comes from your heartfelt belief that you are right in what you ask students to do. The greatest strengths you show to students come from confidence and conviction. Smile every day and be clear on your limits. Most new teachers have more internal strength than they realize. They just need to search within themselves to find it. Be sure never to do anything that you don't want students to do. Don't manipulate; don't make threats you can't back up; don't lie. Most important, develop confidence by being prepared. Students see lack of confidence, more than anything else, as a sign that you are a target.

Brian: It is not about starting out tough. It is about caring more than anyone has cared. It is about creating strong, sound lessons kids can relate to. It is about being real. It is about sharing personal struggles and success. It is also about saying no sometimes. Instead of focusing on being mean or nice, focus on constantly teaching. Whether it is academics or behavior, just teach all the time and make lives better. Do this and you will be fine.

Allen: You can be tough and respectful without being mean: You should have clear procedures and expectations. In fact, spend the first few days—maybe even the first few weeks—making this your top priority. Practice how you expect students to enter the room, talk to each other, express disagreement, seek approval to use the bathroom, and so on. Involve them in the formal discipline plan of values, rules, and consequences (Chapter 6). Let them know how and when you plan to handle misbehavior if it occurs. When it does happen, use it as an opportunity to confront it firmly but respectfully; for example, "We don't say that here. Maybe you forgot, but in this class we ask permission before we get out of our seats." Most important is to let students know that their success is your top goal and to be sure that your policies and procedures guarantee their success if they prepare, plan, practice, and persist.

Why do some kids behave perfectly for certain adults and badly for others? What is one teacher doing that the others are not?

Brian: Building relationships. Always. Building anything that is valuable never happens quickly. Building takes time, energy, effort, care, and patience. Learn to really listen. Ask questions, make predictions, read minds, and always seek to connect.

Here are some other things you can do:

• **Make time.** Very few schools build time into the schedule for relationship building. Our job is to create time in the classroom or find time outside it.

• **Summon your energy.** Challenging students are great at draining energy. Sometimes we give ourselves a "pregame pep talk" before working with them. Do whatever it takes.

• **Make an effort.** How hard have you really tried? Some teachers tell us, "I have this student and I have tried everything." Have you called her at home? Have you complimented her privately? Have you told her how much you care? What exactly does "everything" mean? Have you taken five minutes every day to walk around the school with her, talking about anything other than school?

• **Practice being a great explainer.** Great explainers talk a student into or out of most behaviors. They show the student how it is in his best interest to complete a task. Practice the skill of explaining!

• **Become great at reading people.** Do you notice when people are happy, mad, glad, sad, or aggravated—without their saying a word? How long does it take you to notice? Noticing body language is a crucial element to building a relationship. Sometimes it is important to back off and give the student some space.

• **Push boundaries.** Ask questions others are not willing to ask. Tell students how they are feeling even if they do not admit it. Ask about students' home lives and tell them about struggles you had as a child. Again, the goal is to relate.

Allen: In addition to relationships, the requirements of a subject area and a child's capacity to achieve success are critically important. The greater the spread between these two variables, the greater the chance of challenging behavior, even with teachers who are great at relationship building. If an 8th grader has 3rd grade–level math skills, even teachers with the best interpersonal skills who care deeply about the student are likely to see inappropriate behavior unless modifications are made to the curriculum.

There is one other important and often misunderstood dynamic that influences how a child behaves in the presence of different adults. It is very common for children to show their worst behavior where they feel safest—as exemplified by the parent who gets surly, uncooperative behavior from her child but great reports about the child from everyone else. Children are most apt to test limits where they feel most comfortable.

Finally, kids who have experienced rejection are unlikely to trust the affection shown by a caring teacher. They begin to trust only after realizing that the caring is genuine, so they test by displaying negative behavior. If the teacher is stronger than the student in not giving up, there is often an important breakthrough that can last a lifetime.

Rick: Students respond better to teachers who are genuine, don't try to manipulate, and tell the truth straight-up. Students react differently to teachers who take on roles that are not genuine, who manipulate rather than are straightforward, and who humiliate them.

What is the best tip for quickly defusing a student's escalating negative behavior?

Brian: Focus on two words guaranteed to defuse most situations, anywhere, at any time: "I'm sorry." Don't be afraid to say them, and say them with genuine feeling. You may need to repeat the words over and over until the student calms down. Learn to say "I'm sorry" even if you feel you did nothing wrong. You can follow "I'm sorry I said or did something to get you so mad" with "Maybe you can tell me what I did so I won't make the same mistake again." Next, put yourself on the same "team" as the student by talking about how similar you are. For example, "I make mistakes; so do you. I sometimes call people names, just like you. I'm sometimes impulsive, just like you. The best I can do is apologize for my mistake. Now that you know how I feel, is there anything you think you can do differently next time?" Once a student views you as a teammate, you can coach him. The next phase is to give the specific strategies to use when angry and then to practice.

Allen: Remain steady and calm. *Acknowledge* the student's frustration or anger ("I can see you are very upset right now"), show *agreement* ("There's probably a lot you have to say about that"), *defer* ("It's really important that I listen and understand. I promise I will after the lesson"), show *appreciation* for waiting ("Thanks for hanging in until then. I know it's tough to wait"). (See Chapter 7 for other informal methods of dealing with student misbehavior.)

Can oppositional defiance be changed?

Brian: Yes, oppositional defiance can be changed by challenging students and using questions instead of statements. Almost everyone likes a challenge—as long as it can actually be accomplished. If the ability to succeed is not there, challenge only leads to annoyance and frustration. So this strategy comes with a stern warning: use it only if what you challenge the student to do is something he can accomplish.

It is important to remember the nature of oppositional students. Most argue and disagree just for the purpose of arguing and disagreeing. When we challenge a student, the message we send is that we do not believe he has the ability to succeed, even though we know he really does. Here is an example of using challenge to get a student to complete homework. Say to the entire class, "Tonight for homework, please write an essay. I want to see your completed essays tomorrow. Have a great night." Then pull the oppositional student aside and say, "Did you hear what I said to the class? Unfortunately, I highly doubt I will see an essay from you tomorrow. Good luck proving me wrong." Then walk away.

This approach does not always work. However, because the student is oppositional, he will often do the right thing just to prove the teacher wrong. If he does not complete the homework, he proves the teacher correct. For oppositional students, proving a teacher correct is often the worst thing they can do.

This strategy is not often used because it is not often taught. You can adopt "challenge" phrases for more success with oppositional students. Here are some examples:

- "Yesterday you did three problems. That's good. I wonder if you can complete all five tonight. We shall see."
- "Great job with the reading assignment. It is hard to believe you will be able to complete it two nights in a row. We will see tomorrow!"
- "Who can't behave for one day? It would be much more impressive if you could act the same way tomorrow. Is it possible? Good luck!"

You can also use questions. Pick one day, and from start to finish, only use questions in your interactions with the student, and see what happens. Here are some examples:

Student: What's the consequence going to be?
Teacher: What will it take for you to stop calling people names?

Student: Why do we have to do this work?
Teacher: Why do *you* think this work needs to get done? Can you explain to us?

Questions are kryptonite for oppositional students.

Allen: The only thing you can't change is your DNA. That said, we devote an entire chapter in this book to "change" because it usually isn't easy (see Chapter 4). Like driving a car on a road weathered with bumps and potholes after a long winter, the ride is rarely smooth and often uncertain. Although a smidgen of "oppositional defiance" is necessary to become "strong-willed," kids with too much display this kind of behavior because they need it to feel they are in control. Reducing it means showing them healthy ways to feel in control. You can try lots of ways to do that, such as assigning them to valued classroom jobs and responsibilities or involving them directly in developing rules and consequences; but it is important to keep in mind that almost always, these kids will repeatedly revisit their old behaviors until the new ones provide them the same sense of security. It is difficult but necessary to not get discouraged when you hit a pothole.

Rick: In Chapter 7 we describe the process of reframing. Start by reframing "opposition" as "refusing to give up." Show admiration for that quality, and help the student discover other, more productive ways to use it. In Chapter 10 we describe a strategy called "behaving paradoxically." If a student refuses to do what you want, tell him to do what he wants. This sounds strange, but if he won't do what you say, then he won't do what he wants to do simply because you told him to do it.

References

Alge, C. (2015, November 2). Celebrating (instead of faulting) failure: 8 companies that glorify their flops [blog post]. *LexTalk*. Retrieved from https://www.lextalk.com/b/lextalk_blog/archive/2015/11/02/celebrating-instead-of-faulting-failure-8-companies-that-glorify-their-flops.aspx

American Psychiatric Association. (2013). *Diagnostic and statistical manual of mental disorders (DSM—5)*. Washington DC: American Psychiatric Association.

Amurao, C. (2013). Fact sheet: How bad is the school-to-prison pipeline? *Tavis Smiley Reports*. Retrieved from http://www.pbs.org/wnet/tavissmiley/tsr/education-under-arrest/school-to-prison-pipeline-fact-sheet/

Antoniou, A. S., Polychroni, P., & Vlachakis, A. N. (2006). Gender and age differences in occupational stress and professional burnout between primary and high-school teachers in Greece. *Journal of Managerial Psychology, 21*(7), 682–690.

Bergmann, J., & Sams, A. (2012). *Flip your classroom: Reach every student in every class every day*. Alexandria, VA: ASCD.

Bureau of Labor Statistics. (2016). Employment projections. Washington, DC: United States Department of Labor. Retrieved from http://www.bls.gov/emp/ep_chart_001.htm

Camp, B. W., Blom, G. E., Herbert, F., & Van Doorninck, W. J. (1977). Think aloud: A program for developing self-control in young aggressive boys. *Journal of Abnormal Child Psychology, 5*, 157–169.

Christian, S. (2003). *Educating children in foster care*. Washington, DC: Children's Policy Initiative. Retrieved from http://www.ncsl.org/programs/cyf/cpieducate.pdf

Crow, K., & Ward-Lonergan, J. (2003). *An analysis of personal event narratives produced by school age children.* Paper presented at the annual meeting of the Council for Exceptional Children, New York. (ERIC Documentation Reproduction Service No. ED 481 292). Retrieved from http://www.eric.ed.gov/ERICDocs/data/ericdocs2sql/content_storage_01/0000019b/80/1b/74/98.pdf

Cszikszentmihalyi, M. (1990). *Flow: The psychology of optimal experience.* New York: Harper & Row.

Curwin, R. (2010). *Meeting students where they live: Motivation in urban schools.* Alexandria VA: ASCD.

Curwin, R. (2017). How to respond when students use hate speech [blog post]. *Edutopia.* Retrieved from https://www.edutopia.org/blog/how-respond-when-students-use-hate-speech-richard-curwin

Curwin, R., & Mendler, A. (1988). *Discipline with dignity* (1st ed.). Alexandria, VA: ASCD.

David, D. S. (2009). *Mindful teaching and teaching mindfulness: A guide for anyone who teaches anything.* Somerville, MA: Wisdom Publications.

Ellis, J., Small-McGinley, J., & De Fabrizio, L. (1999). It's so great to have an adult friend: A teacher-student mentorship program for at-risk youth. *Reaching Today's Youth, 3*(4), 46–50.

Feindler, E. L., & Ecton, R. B. (1986). *Adolescent anger control: Cognitive-behavioral techniques.* New York: Pergamon.

Fisher, G. (2007, April 9). Amputee looks at his new life as "another chance"; Arizona teacher is inspiration after loss of four limbs. *USA Today,* p. 4D.

Frankl, V. (1963/2006). *Man's search for meaning.* Boston: Beacon Press.

Gallup. (2014). *State of American schools: The path to winning again in education.* Retrieved from http://www.gallup.com/services/178709/state-america-schools-report.aspx

Gladwell, M. (2016, June 29). The big man can't shoot [podcast]. *Revisionist History.* Retrieved from http://revisionisthistory.com/episodes/03-the-big-man-cant-shoot

Goldstein, A. (1999). *The prepared curriculum: Teaching prosocial competencies.* Champaign, IL: Research Press.

Greenburg, M. T., Brown, J. L., & Abenavoli, R. M. (2016, September 1). *Teacher stress and health effects on teachers, students, and schools* [issue brief]. University Park, PA: Edna Bennett Pierce Prevention Research Center, Pennsylvania State University.

Haupt, A. (2016, December 8). Mindfulness in schools: When meditation replaces detention. *U.S. News & World Report.* Retrieved from http://health.usnews.com/wellness/mind/articles/2016-12-08/mindfulness-in-schools-when-meditation-replaces-detention

Hauser, C. (2017, February 8). Teenagers who vandalized historic black schoolhouse are ordered to read books. *New York Times.* Retrieved from https://www.nytimes.com/2017/02/08/us/black-school-racist-sexist-graffiti.html

Henley, M. (2003). *Teaching self-control.* Bloomington, IN: Solution Tree.

Holtham, J. (2009). *Taking restorative justice to schools: A doorway to discipline.* Allen, TX: Del Hayes Press.

Jennings, P. A., & Siegel, D. J. (2015). *Mindfulness for teachers: Simple skills for peace and productivity in the classroom.* New York: W. W. Norton.

Jensen, E. (2000). *Different brains, different learners: How to reach the hard to reach.* Thousand Oaks, CA: Corwin.

Kavilanz, P. (2017). Teachers welcome standing desks in the classroom. *CNN Money.* Retrieved from http://money.cnn.com/2017/01/10/smallbusiness/jaswig-standing-desk-schools/index.html

Kneebone, E., & Holmes, N. (2016). *U.S. concentrated poverty in the wake of the Great Recession.* Washington, DC: Brookings Institutions. Retrieved from https://www.

brookings.edu/research/u-s-concentrated-poverty-in-the-wake-of-the-great-recession/

Lane, K. L., Kalberg, J. R., & Menzies, H. M. (2009). *Developing school-wide programs to prevent and manage problem behaviors.* New York: Guilford Press.

Levinson, W., Roter, D. L., Mullooly, J. P., Dull, V. T., & Frankel, R. M. (1997). Physician-patient communication. *JAMA, 277*(7), 553–559.

Loomans, D., & Kolberg, K. (2002). *The laughing classroom: Everyone's guide to teaching with humor* (2nd ed.). Tiburon, CA: H. J. Kramer.

Lundberg, E., & Thurston, C. M. (2002). *If they're laughing, they just might be listening: Ideas for using humor effectively in the classroom.* Tiburon, CA: H. J. Kramer.

Maltese, A. V., Tai, R. H., & Fan, X. (2012, October–November). When is homework worth the time? *High School Journal, 96*(1), 52–72.

Martin, J. A., Hamilton, B. E., Osterman, M. J. K., Driscoll, A. K., & Mathews, T. J. (2017, January 5). Births: Final data for 2015. *National Vital Statistics Reports, 66*(1). Atlanta, GA: Centers for Disease Control. Retrieved from https://www.cdc.gov/nchs/data/nvsr/nvsr66/nvsr66_01.pdf

May, R. (1969). *Love and will.* New York: W. W. Norton.

Meichenbaum, D. (1977). *Cognitive behavior modification.* New York: Plenum.

Meier, D. (2013, April 11). Explaining KIPP's SLANT [blog post]. *Education Week.* Retrieved from http://blogs.edweek.org/edweek/Bridging-Differences/2013/04/Slant_and_the_golden_rule.html

Mendler, A. N. (2005). *More what do I do when: Powerful strategies to promote positive behavior.* Bloomington, IN: Solution Tree.

Mendler, A. N. (2012). *When teaching gets tough: Smart ways to reclaim your game.* Alexandria, VA: ASCD.

Mendler, A. N. (2014). *The resilient teacher.* Alexandria, VA: ASCD.

Mendler, A. N., & Mendler, B. D. (2017). *Turning tough parents into strong partners.* Rochester, NY: Teacher Learning Center.

Mendler, B., Curwin, R., & Mendler, A. (2008). *Strategies for successful classroom management.* Thousand Oaks, CA: Corwin.

Molnar, A., & Linquist, B. (1990). *Changing problem behavior in schools.* San Francisco: Jossey-Bass.

Moscowitz, F., & Hayman J. L. (1974). Interaction patterns of first year, typical and "best" teachers in inner-city schools. *Journal of Educational Research, 67,* 224–230.

Ogoe, R. (2015). The kinetic classroom: The pedal-desk, ADHD, and the mind-body connection [blog post]. Center for Educational Improvement. Retrieved from http://www.edimprovement.org/2015/06/kinetic-classroom-pedal-desk-adhd-mind-body-connection/

PBS. (2016). Interview with Richard Dreyfuss. *Tavis Smiley Show.* Retrieved from http://www.pbs.org/wnet/tavissmiley/interviews/actor-richard-dreyfuss-2/

Pearson Foundation. (2014). Survey reveals what students really think of teachers [blog post]. *Teaching Community.* Retrieved from http://teaching.monster.com/benefits/articles/7007-survey-reveals-what-students-really-think-of-teachers

Peri, C. (2011). *Teenagers educated the village way.* Englewood, NJ: This World: The Values Network Publishing Group.

Potter, D. (2010). Psychosocial well-being and the relationship between divorce and children's academic achievement. *Journal of Marriage and Family, 72,* 933, 940–941.

Potter, H. (2013, May). Boosting achievement by pursuing diversity. *Educational Leadership, 70*(8), 38–43. Retrieved from http://www.ascd.org/publications/educational-leadership/may13/vol70/num08/Boosting-Achievement-by-Pursuing-Diversity.aspx

Quinlan, C. (2016, June 7). New data shows the school-to-prison pipeline starts as early as preschool. ThinkProgress. Retrieved from https://thinkprogress.org/new-data-shows-the-school-to-prison-pipeline-starts-as-early-as-preschool-80fc1c3e85be/

Ratey, J. J. (2013). *Spark: The revolutionary new source of exercise and the brain.* New York: Little, Brown.

Rich, S. (2007). *Ant farm.* New York: Random House.

Rogers, K. (2015, December 21). Oberlin students take culture war to the dining hall. *New York Times.* Retrieved from https://www.nytimes.com/2015/12/22/us/oberlin-takes-culture-war-to-the-dining-hall.html

Shaw, J. (2016). New Orleans high school turbocharges restorative justice. *Hechinger Report.* Retrieved from http://hechingerreport.org/new-orleans-high-school-turbocharges-restorative-justice/

Shirley, D., & MacDonald, E. (2016). *The mindful teacher.* New York: Teachers College Press.

Sweeney, A., & Gorner, J. (2016, July 1). 10 shootings a day: Complex causes of Chicago's spiking violence. *Chicago Tribune.* Retrieved from http://www.chicagotribune.com/news/ct-chicago-shootings-violence-2016-met-20160630-story.html

U.S. Centers for Disease Control and Prevention. (2016). Autism spectrum disorder: Data & statistics. Retrieved from https://www.cdc.gov/ncbddd/autism/data.html

Visser, S. N., Danielson, M. L., Bitsko, R. H., et al. (2014). Trends in the parent-report of health care provider-diagnosed and medicated attention-deficit/hyperactivity disorder: United States, 2003–2011. *Journal of the American Academy of Child & Adolescent Psychiatry, 53*(1), 34–46. Retrieved from http://www.jaacap.com/article/S0890-8567(13)00594-7/abstract

Wang, M. C., Haertel, G. D., & Walberg, H. J. (1997). Fostering educational resilience in inner-city schools. *Children and Youth, 7,* 119–140.

Watson, Z. (2014, October 28). 4 real-world examples that explain intrinsic motivation [blog post]. *Technology Advice.* Retrieved from http://technologyadvice.com/blog/marketing/4-real-world-examples-clearly-explain-intrinsic-motivation/

Weiner, B. (1972). Attribution theory, achievement motivation, and the educational process. *Review of Educational Research, 42*(2), 203–215.

Wendt, M. (2002, Fall). Can exercise replace medication as a treatment for ADHD? *Healing Magazine, 78.*

Werner, E. E., & Smith, R. S. (1989). *Vulnerable but invincible: A longitudinal study of resilient children and youth.* New York: Adams.

Wilson, D., & Conyers, M. (2013). *Five big ideas for effective teaching: Research to classroom practice.* New York: Teachers College Press.

Wineburg, S. (2013, November 14). Changing the teaching of history, one byte at a time [blog post]. *Edutopia.* Retrieved from https://www.edutopia.org/blog/changing-the-teaching-of-history-sam-wineburg

Zillgitt, J. (2017, June 13). LeBron James' legacy secure despite NBA finals loss to Warriors. *USA Today.* Retrieved from https://www.usatoday.com/story/sports/nba/playoffs/2017/06/13/cavs-lebron-james-legacy-secure-nba-finals-loss-warriors/102803736/

Index

About the Authors

 **Dr. Richard L. Curwin** is an author, speaker, and experienced practitioner who explores issues of student discipline, behavioral management, and motivation. During his 45 years in the classroom, he served as a 7th grade educator, teacher of emotionally disturbed children, college professor, and director of the graduate program for disabled youth at David Yellin College in Jerusalem. The behavior management strategies and philosophies he shares have worked for parents and educators throughout the world. With his colleague Dr. Allen N. Mendler, Dr. Curwin founded Discipline Associates, created the Discipline with Dignity program, and coauthored *Discipline with Dignity for Challenging Youth* and *As Tough as Necessary: Countering Violence, Aggression, and Hostility in Our Schools*. He is also the author of *Am I in Trouble: Using Discipline to Teach Young Children Responsibility; Rediscovering Hope: Our Greatest Teaching Strategy; Making Good Choices: Developing Responsibility, Respect, and Self-Discipline in Grades 4–9; Motivating Students Left Behind;* and *Meeting Students Where They Live: Motivation in Urban Schools*. He is the recipient of the Spirit of Crazy Horse Award, presented by Reclaiming Youth International, for his courage in reaching discouraged youth. He has appeared on several podcasts and the *Today Show,* and he is a regular editorial writer for the *Jerusalem Post* and a blogger for *Edutopia*. He can be reached at richardcurwin@gmail.com.

Dr. Allen N. Mendler is an educator and school psychologist with extensive experience working with children of all ages in regular education and special education settings. Dr. Mendler's emphasis is on developing effective frameworks and strategies for educators, youth professionals, and parents to help youth with learning and behavior problems succeed. As a motivational speaker and trainer on topics pertaining to challenging students, he has given workshops and seminars around the world. He is the author or coauthor of numerous books and publications, including *Discipline with Dignity, The Resilient Teacher, When Teaching Gets Tough, Connecting with Students, Motivating Students Who Don't Care,* and the *What Do I Do When* series. He blogs frequently for *Edutopia* and other online publications and has presented numerous webinars on such topics as power struggles, bullying, motivating and managing difficult students, and teaching self-control. Dr. Mendler has been recognized by the Bureau of Education and Research (BER) for his excellence in teaching, and he is a recipient of the Spirit of Crazy Horse Award, awarded by Reclaiming Youth International, for his contributions to improving the lives of discouraged youth. He can be reached at almendler@gmail.com or on Twitter at @allenmendler.

Brian D. Mendler has extensive experience working with challenging students in general education, self-contained, and inclusion settings. He provides staff development training for K–12 educators throughout the world, drawing upon his own experiences as a student who struggled with a learning disability and severe ADHD, and focusing on how to be successful with even the most difficult students. Mr. Mendler is the author of *That One Kid,* providing educators with strategies for preventing and responding to difficult, disruptive, defiant, and unmotivated behavior, and *The Taming of the Crew.* He is also a coauthor of *Turning Tough Parents into Strong Partners, Strategies for Successful Classroom Management, Power Struggles* (2nd edition), and *Discipline with Dignity* (3rd edition). He can be reached on Twitter and Instagram at @BrianMendler.

Related ASCD Resources

At the time of publication, the following resources were available (ASCD stock numbers appear in parentheses).

PD Online® Courses
Classroom Management: Managing Challenging Behavior, 2nd Edition (#PD14OC015)

Understanding Student Motivation, 2nd Edition (#PD11OC106M)

Print Products
Better Than Carrots or Sticks: Restorative Practices for Positive Classroom Management by Dominique Smith, Douglas B. Fisher, and Nancy E. Frey (#116005)

Doing Poorly on Purpose: Strategies to Reverse Underachievement and Respect Student Dignity by James R. Delisle (#118023)

Fostering Resilient Learners: Strategies for Creating a Trauma-Sensitive Classroom by Kristin Souers with Pete Hall (#116014)

Handling Student Frustrations: How Do I Help Students Manage Emotions in the Classroom? (ASCD Arias) by Renate Caine and Carol McClintic (#SF114068)

Hanging In: Strategies for Teaching the Students Who Challenge Us Most by Jeffrey Benson (#114013)

Inspiring the Best in Students by Jonathan C. Erwin (#110006)

Meeting Students Where They Live: Motivation in Urban Schools by Richard L. Curwin (#109110)

For up-to-date information about ASCD resources, go to www.ascd.org. You can search the complete archives of *Educational Leadership* at www.ascd.org/el.

ASCD EDge® Group
Exchange ideas and connect with other educators on the social networking site ASCD EDge at http://ascdedge.ascd.org/.

ASCD myTeachSource®
Download resources from a professional learning platform with hundreds of research-based best practices and tools for your classroom at http://myteachsource.ascd.org/.

For more information, send an e-mail to member@ascd.org; call 1-800-933-2723 or 703-578-9600; send a fax to 703-575-5400; or write to Information Services, ASCD, 1703 N. Beauregard St., Alexandria, VA 22311-1714 USA.